BEYOND EMOJIS

8 SIMPLE STRATEGIES FOR TEENS TO IMPROVE RELATIONSHIPS, REDUCE MISUNDERSTANDINGS, AND NAVIGATE CHALLENGING DIGITAL SITUATIONS

ALEXANDER VAUGHN

CONTENTS

INTRODUCTION

Can you think of a time when you don't use or look at your smartphone? Take a few seconds to reflect on what you did today. You probably woke up in the morning, turned off your phone's alarm, and looked at your notifications. Therefore, one of the first things you do in the morning is look at your smartphone. If your best friend texted you, you might feel the need to reply as soon as possible. If you see some funny memes or cute pictures on your social media, you might leave a like or comment. From that moment onward, you might never stop looking at your notifications. You get out of bed, have breakfast, answer your best friend who replied to you in the meantime, and leave another like or comment. You go to school and check if someone replied to your messages or texted you on one of your dozens of groups. It looks like a vicious circle with no end. A new message or comment leads to another message or comment, and so on. Finally, the day ends, and you go to bed. You probably check your smartphone one last time and close your eyes. If you're lucky and turn your phone on mute, you won't be disturbed by notifications. If you struggle to fall asleep and can see your phone light up, you might stay awake all night to scroll through social media and text your friends.

Do you recognize yourself in the above scenario? What's your typical day? Do you manage not to look at your phone while you're in class, doing your homework, or maybe having dinner with your family? If not, you're not different from your peers. Many studies have tried to analyze the frequency with which teens use social media and found interesting results. A survey conducted from 2014 to 2015 discovered that 24% of teens reported using their smartphones almost constantly (Anderson & Jiang, 2018). In 2018, the same survey was conducted again, and the number of participants reporting using their smartphones almost constantly doubled (45%). Can you imagine how the percentage might have changed in the last few years?

Now, ask yourself one simple question: *Would I be able to turn my phone off or not use it for a few hours or even a whole day?* You might automatically reply that you're perfectly able to avoid social media, WhatsApp, and everything else for a few hours. But have you ever done it? If the answer is "No," then you might overestimate your control over the technology you use daily. You might convince yourself you have the power to disconnect whenever you feel like it and still struggle to do it. You might tell yourself you'll turn your phone off later or the next day and never actually do it.

Now, let's go a bit deeper. How would you define your relationship with social media? Would you say they improve or worsen your life? You might believe that new technologies and social media have many advantages, like making you feel more connected with others, helping you meet a lot of different people online, keeping you updated with everything that happens around the world, and making you feel less lonely. At the same time, you might be aware of the disadvantages, like feeling trapped in the vicious circle described above, feeling the need to always be connected, enduring strangers' judgment, and struggling to create deep and lasting relationships. But that's not all. All adults and people older than you define your generation as native to the digital realm and consider you capable of handling all sorts of issues. In reality, you grapple every day with a unique set of challenges. You try to read between the lines, detect nuances, and build genuine connections without essential physical cues, like the tone of voice or facial expressions. How can you be sure that an emoji has the same meaning for you and your friend? What if they interpret it differently and misunderstand what you want to tell them? I guess it happened at least once in your life.

So, how can you deepen your knowledge of social media, learn to properly use it, and feel better about yourself? The answer is here, in this book. You might believe you already know everything about social media and don't need anybody's help, or that books are not the best means to show how new technology works. You might also think you have no time to read and the information you find in this book will be outdated before you finish it. If you keep reading, you might find out you're not as tech-savvy as you thought, and books aren't as boring as you believed. Do you want to test this hypothesis?

"Beyond Emojis" is a straightforward handbook that will help you strengthen your communication skills through eight practical strategies you'll discover in the following eight chapters. Chapter 1 helps you understand the digital landscape and why it matters. Chapter 2 focuses on the nuances of texts, how online communication can be multifaceted, and how misinterpretations and misunderstandings can arise. Chapter 3 shows the pros and cons of emojis and how people use them to represent emotions. Chapter 4 teaches you the importance of empathy and why and how you can develop it online. Chapter 5 focuses on online conflicts: How they arise, how you can solve them, and how you can perceive them positively. Chapter 6 concerns relationships and the most effective ways of developing good online and offline friendships. Chapter 7 deals with an apparently boring but essential topic: Digital etiquette. You'll discover what it is and why it's important. Finally, Chapter 8 helps you avoid digital perfectionism and become more authentic in your online interactions. In all the above chapters, you'll find a theoretical part followed by a practical, easy activity linked with the main topic that will help you become more aware of your digital presence and how you use your smartphone to communicate.

As a communication expert and author, I met many teenagers during my life. I've always been curious about how technology changes their daily lives and impacts their emotions. With an expansive background in tech and education, I've always helped teens achieve effective communication through social media. At this point in human history, saying things like, "Social media and smartphones are bad, we must ban them, and our kids must never use them," is completely useless. Social media are here and won't go away soon, so we'd better get used to and take advantage of them. I put all my effort into making this book as engaging and practical as possible to ensure you're well-equipped to express yourself confidently and safely online. Here, you'll find all the information I gathered over the years through extensive research and hands-on experience.

"Beyond Emojis" is not just a handbook; it's an experience. It challenges you to question, reflect, and evolve, ensuring that your digital footprint is one of understanding, respect, and genuine connection. Step into a world where every message you send resonates, every online interaction strengthens relationships, and where you're empowered to bridge the gap between emojis and emotions. Dive deep, go beyond, and discover the art and heart of digital communication.

1

NAVIGATING THE DIGITAL LANDSCAPE

The single biggest problem in communication is the illusion that it has taken place.

— GEORGE BERNARD SHAW

D o you really know what the digital landscape is? If you think you have all the answers and digital communication has no secrets, then get ready to see things from a new perspective. In this chapter, we'll discuss the first strategy you can use to improve your digital communication: Knowing more about it. We'll discover what digital communication is, its outlets, and its benefits. Next, we'll discuss the main disadvantages and pitfalls of communicating online and why digital communication is essential in our modern society. At the end of the chapter, you'll also find a practical activity to analyze your digital communication and understand how much you really know about it.

WHAT IS DIGITAL COMMUNICATION?

Defining Communication

Let's start with the basics. What is communication? Communication is a simple act we all engage in every day of our lives, almost all moments. When you communicate something, you send a message to someone else to express your feelings or share your opinion. Communicating is the act of transferring information from one individual to another. The main elements of communication are three and are very easy to understand: Sender, recipient, and message (*What Is Communication?*, 2011). The sender sends the message (or information) to the recipient who interprets it. It looks as easy as drinking a glass of water. But is it in practice?

In most cases, we don't communicate what we really think and feel because of various internal and external factors. Internal factors include our emotions, culture, and background, which influence the way we talk. External factors include the recipient's emotions, culture, and background, and the environment where the communication occurs. If we try to talk with someone in a crowded place with a lot of noise, it's more likely that we won't effectively interact with them. The same is true when we're surrounded by distractions, like smartphones and other devices, music, other people, and everything that can divert our attention away from our conversations.

In fact, communication is an active process that involves both the sender and recipient at the same level. If the sender can't convey a clear message, then the recipient won't understand what they want from them. At the same time, if the recipient isn't listening, the sender won't be able to express their ideas and feelings. Therefore, they must both be present and fully engaged in the conversation to make sure that the sender manages to send their message and the recipient receives and understands it. Then, the recipient answers to the sender's message, and they automatically switch their roles. Communication looks a bit more difficult now, doesn't it? And it gets even worse when more than two people are interacting at the same time. I guess you have probably found yourself in a situation where you were speaking with your friends, and you all talked over each other or drowned each other out. Similar circumstances can often occur in our lives if we don't know the importance of conveying the right message and listening to others.

Digital Communication Outlets

Now, you get an idea of how hard digital communication can be. At least, in real life, you have some physical clues you can look at to better understand what others are saying. For example, you can look at their facial expressions and posture, or listen to their tone of voice. Online, you don't even have such fundamental clues. The online world is so complicated and multifaceted that effectively communicating what we have inside looks almost impossible. Just think about the fact that you can use various tools to interact with people online: Apps, emails, and text.

Nowadays, we have plenty of communication apps we can choose from. If we want to rapidly send a message to our friends, we can use WhatsApp or Telegram. If we want to see them even if they're far away from us, we can use Microsoft Teams, Zoom, or Skype. All the above apps help us communicate with people around the world and send messages instantly. You might have probably used Microsoft Teams or similar apps to follow your online lessons during the COVID-19 pandemic, so you have an idea of how they work. Otherwise, companies use Slack, Asana, and similar tools to organize and manage their work and give employees the possibility to exchange information online. As useful as all the above apps might appear, they have some serious cons. They're not completely secure, so you must pay attention to your personal data. They require a stable internet connection, and they might replace face-to-face interactions, thus hindering people's communication skills.

Emails are a common means of communication that are particularly helpful when you're in college or at work. However, misinterpretations and misunderstandings can easily happen if you don't manage to effectively convey your message. An email is appropriate when you can't reach the person via telephone, or you can't meet them for one reason or another. It's also appropriate when you don't need an urgent response, have to send electronic files, or need a written record of the conversation. An email isn't appropriate when you have to convey a long and complex message (in that case, it's better to meet them face-to-face) and when the content of your email is emotionally charged.

Moreover, keep in mind that emails are never private, as they can be sent to anyone without you knowing it, so make sure that the content is not highly confidential. Then, always consider the person you want to send the email to and your relationship with them. You might not want to send your professor an email saying something like, "I didn't understand the topic you discussed today in class. Can we talk about it in your office?" To write an effective email, add all the important information that can help the receiver understand what you're talking about, insert a short but explanatory subject line, and close with a greeting.

Finally, the communication outlet that, more than any other, influences our everyday life is text or non-verbal communication. We're not just talking about what you write to your best friend, but how you use social media. Do you know what happens if you like everything you see? One person tried it in an experiment and managed to increase their followers and go to parties more often. At the same time, people recognized them on the street and wanted them to post more (Seiter, 2016). What is the psychology behind social media that makes us crave more? When we like, comment, or share, we increase our dopamine and oxytocin levels, which are two chemicals that make us feel good. Studies have found that social media have such a huge effect on our brains that resisting to tweet is much harder than resisting to smoke or drink alcohol. At the same time, 10 minutes spent on social media correspond to the same arousal people achieve when they get married (Seiter, 2016). Isn't it shocking? Using social media can become an addiction for many reasons. We all want to talk about ourselves, and social media gives us this opportunity while also allowing us to control what we share. When we speak with someone face-to-face, we usually can't manage our emotions nor decide what we want to share, while on social media, it's much easier. Moreover, commenting and liking is a good way of building and maintaining relationships with others.

Benefits

What are the real benefits of digital communication? You witness them every day and might not even notice them. Thanks to digital communication, you can reach anyone you want in the world. If your best friend moves to Europe, you can easily text them on Telegram or make a video call. In fact, another important benefit is that you can communicate in real-time. Before the advancement of technology, people had to send letters by mail and wait for days to get an answer. Now, the moment you send a message, the receiver sees it. Therefore, digital communication is much faster and more efficient than analog one. It's also more convenient, as you don't have to spend money to send a message—you just need an internet connection.

Moreover, digital communication is flexible and accessible, as smartphones don't cost as much as before, and downloading apps like WhatsApp or Instagram is completely free. Therefore, anyone can open an account. Digital communication also has a nonexistent environmental impact because you don't have to use paper or other materials to send texts. Finally, digital communication enhances collaboration and promotes personalization. If you can talk to anyone around the world, you're more likely to establish connections with people who have different backgrounds and cultures. You're also more likely to understand and support them. But digital communication also offers you the opportunity to create your self-image and personalize your messages. Do you have a friend who always uses the same emoji so much that you would recognize their message even without knowing they sent it? This is just an example of how you can use social media to create your self-image and transmit specific messages.

CHALLENGES OF DIGITAL COMMUNICATION FOR TEENS

Why Digital Communication Can Be Confusing

When all people began to have internet access, communication channels were very limited and clear. For example, in the workplace, people used to send emails and expect a reply in less than 24 hours or a business day. That was the rule of thumb, which was generally respected by all coworkers, as there was no other means of communication. Nowadays, you can reach a person in so many ways that you don't know which one to choose. Digital communication can be confusing because we can pick from an infinite number of channels to send messages.

For this reason, you should learn to differentiate them. How can you choose the best channel to send your message? You must consider both privacy and urgency. Privacy is measured by the number of people you want to send the message to. Do you want just your best friend to read it or all your friends, family, and everyone on Instagram? Urgency is measured by time: When would you like to receive a response?

The most urgent and private channel of communication is probably face-to-face communication when you're 100% sure you can choose who will receive your message, and they'll reply immediately. Another urgent and private channel is non-verbal or text communication, where you can send a message instantly. However, you're never sure when the other person will answer you. If they're used to looking at their smartphones often, they might reply in a few minutes; if they're not, they might reply after many hours. Apps can be both private or not, depending on if you decide to send a private message to someone in particular or share something on your public profile. In this case, you can choose the best way to send your message depending on its urgency and level of privacy. If you don't want all your followers to know where you had breakfast last morning, you can send a picture to your best friend and nobody else. If you find an interesting article you want to share with all your friends, you can publish it in your public profile. In both cases, people will reply depending on the amount of time they dedicate to social media. Lastly, emails are not the only digital communication channel anymore, so nobody expects to receive an answer within 24 hours. Nowadays, people who send an email know they can wait for a few days before receiving a response.

Digital communication can also be confusing because we lack essential non-verbal cues that help us understand when someone's listening, agreeing with us, or feeling uncomfortable. When you look at someone face-to-face, you can easily understand how they feel and if they like the conversation. If you notice they rarely look you in the eye and keep focusing on what's happening around them, you have a pretty clear idea that they're not interested in you and what you're saying. It's more difficult to understand someone's feelings and opinions online. The best way to avoid misunderstandings due to the absence of non-verbal cues is to be as clear and concise as you can. Make sure to clearly state how you feel and what you want when you send a message to someone. Do you feel sad because your friend is going out with someone else next weekend? Don't write them, "Okay, go out with whomever you want," but tell them something like, "I thought we were going out together this weekend. I feel sad." (You can also add a sad face if you want). Telling them that they can go out with whoever they want might indicate that you're fine with them meeting other people.

Digital communication might be confusing because it creates a false sense of anonymity and generates expectations of availability and immediacy. We can use nicknames to open social media accounts and write to anyone around the world—people who don't know us and will never meet us in person. Therefore, we might feel like we can write about whatever we want and comment on every post without consequences. However, that's not true. If you want to avoid hurting someone, be responsible and attentive to everything you write. Make sure you don't criticize someone in particular or social groups and that you're always kind and respectful, even when you don't agree with others. Moreover, the idea that you must reply as soon as you can, might impact the quality of your digital communication. The fact that you can always be online and reply in just a few seconds might make you believe that you must answer all the messages you receive. As you'll learn throughout this book, you have every right to answer whenever you want, and nobody forces you to always look at your notifications.

Pitfalls of Communicating Online

Digital communication can also cause common pitfalls. First of all, talking to someone face-to-face requires much more interpersonal skills and a level of intimacy that is impossible to reach through digital communication. Having your first date with the person you like face-to-face or on social media is completely different from being dumped on WhatsApp or in person. If such situations ever happened to you, you know exactly what I'm talking about. Moreover, digital communication requires fewer interpersonal skills than face-to-face interactions, so it doesn't help us develop our emotional intelligence. In other words, feeling empathetic and understanding others is harder. Just think about seeing a cute little kitty on the street or a TikTok video: No matter how much you enjoy the latter, you'll always have more emotional reactions when you see the cat in person. The same is true with people: Seeing someone suffering online doesn't produce the same emotional reaction as doing it face-to-face.

As already mentioned, other common pitfalls of digital communication are misunderstandings and misinterpretations, which easily arise when you can't look at nonverbal cues like body language, facial expressions, and postures. But digital communication also hinders our ability to express ourselves because we have to write how we feel. If you ever had a heated argument with your friends, partner, or family online or tried to tell how you felt over text, you probably know how hard it is. In particular, it isn't easy to stay authentic. Obviously, you can send audio records so that the person you're sending the message to understands your tone of voice and how you feel. Still, you can delete a record and send another one with a different tone of voice and words. Therefore, you can modify your message as much as you want.

Conversely, what you say in person directly comes from your mind, and you don't have a lot of time to carefully choose your words. Finally, digital communication has technical issues that don't occur when talking to someone face-to-face. For example, you might lose connection in the middle of a conversation, or someone might hack your social media accounts and steal private information or send messages without your consent.

IMPORTANCE OF DIGITAL COMMUNICATION IN TODAY'S WORLD

How Digital Communication Benefits Society

Digital communication is important, not just for you and me but for everyone around the world. We already looked at some benefits in the previous sections, but there are many more that interest our whole society. For example, the workplace has completely changed thanks to digital communication. Even before COVID-19, people started working from the comfort of their apartments and going to the office just when it was absolutely necessary. A new type of worker was even born as digital communication advanced: Digital nomads. Digital nomads are all those workers who move around the world however and whenever they want because their job is completely remote so they can work from all countries—they just have to choose the one they prefer living in. Even those workers who aren't digital nomads take advantage of digital communication daily by organizing online meetings, texting their coworkers about the tasks they must accomplish, and sending projects through emails or specific apps.

Digital communication has become so advanced that we can basically do everything with it. Just consider ChatGPT and similar chat-bots that can answer many questions and provide all sorts of information. They're still limited, but they'll probably develop very rapidly and become essential for our everyday life. Thanks to them, everyone can access all information and find an answer to their questions. Although digital communication can give a false sense of anonymity, it also promotes transparency. Whatever you write, comment, like, and share online stays there forever. As you might guess, this has multiple pros and cons. On one hand, it allows you to always check what happens online and go back to see what you shared years before. On the other hand, it means you must pay attention to what you write as anybody can look at it in the future. Even when you're 50 or 70, you'll still be able to look at what you wrote when you were just 16 or 17.

Examples of Digital Communication in Action

Did you get an idea of how beneficial digital communication is in our world? If not, here you find some real-life examples that will help you understand the importance of online communication in our daily lives. Nowadays, many online businesses have live chats that you can use to ask simple questions and solve problems rapidly. Have you ever used one because you couldn't buy something online or had some technical issue you couldn't solve by yourself? I guess so. Live chats are efficient because you can ask for help and get it rapidly. Before live chats existed, people always had to call a number and wait in line for hours to solve even the simplest problems. Another example of the significance of digital communication consists of talking to your loved ones even if they're far away from you. It doesn't matter where your best friend goes on holiday with their family —you can always know where they are and what they're doing. You can text them and receive an answer in a few seconds, or you can look at their social media profiles and see if they posted a new picture. You can also make a video call and see what they're doing in real-time. These are just a few examples, but I'm sure you can think of many more that occur in your everyday life.

DIY

How much do you know about the way you communicate online? Test yourself!

- Gather a list of social media posts, texts, or emails from friends and family.
- Analyze them for tone, context, and emotional cues.
- Consider what might be inferred beyond the words.
- Reflect on any differences in how you perceive digital messages compared to face-to-face communication.

This activity will help you become more aware of how you communicate and how others interpret your texts.

In this chapter, we learned what digital communication is, its various benefits, and its different channels. We also discovered that choosing the right channel is essential to make the receiver understand what we mean and want. Then, we looked at some common challenges and pitfalls that we must face every day to communicate online, such as misinterpretations and misunderstandings. In Chapter 2, we'll keep discussing such challenges, and we'll focus on texts. We'll analyze tone and context and how we can improve our digital communication.

2

THE NUANCES OF TEXT

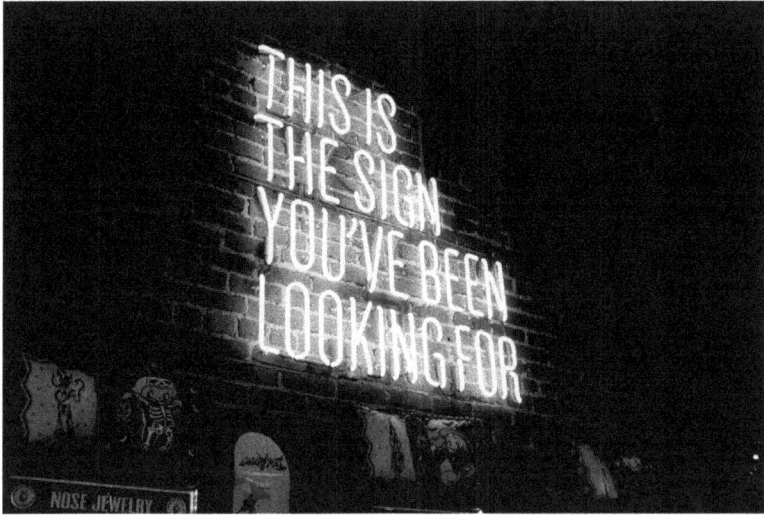

> *Excellent communication doesn't just happen naturally. It is a product of process, skill, climate, relationship and hard work.*

— PAT MCMILLAN

Digital communication can be confusing, as texts can have various nuances. Nuances are subtle or minor things that can often go unnoticed but have a great impact on conversations. That's why it's essential to be aware of all the nuances texts can have, how to spot them, and how to interpret them. This chapter discusses the second strategy you can use to improve your digital communication: Mastering the ability to understand tone and context in online interactions. In the next sections, you'll discover what tone and context are and how they usually get lost in digital communication. You'll deepen your knowledge of misinterpretations and misunderstandings, and you'll learn how to read between the lines. At the end of the chapter, you'll find a practical activity to better understand how tone and context work.

TONE AND CONTEXT: LOST MESSENGERS

What Are the Tone and Context

Did you know that the most important part of communication is non-verbal? To understand the message others convey to us, we mainly use non-verbal cues (Russell, 2021). This means that tone and context are more important than the actual words we write or say. The tone corresponds to the way you get your message across and can be formal or informal, professional or casual, emotional or factual, and so on. For example, your tone can be informal and casual with your friends and professional and factual with your teachers. The tone you use is strictly dependent on word choice, as you'll choose different words according to the message you want to convey and the tone you want to use. Let's say you feel angry with your parents because they tried looking at your smartphone. If you use a formal tone, you might say something like, "Mom, Dad, I feel angry because you looked at my phone without my permission. I would appreciate it if you'd never do it again, please." This tone conveys the message that you feel calm and your parents' actions didn't affect you much. If you want to make them understand you feel frustrated by what they did, you might prefer a different word choice and tone, like "Never look at my phone again! I don't want you to look at my messages!" As you might guess, the tone completely changes the message you convey.

The tone is strictly connected with context. The context concerns your surroundings and everything that happens around you. Imagine being in a library full of kid's books. According to the context, you probably don't expect to find horror or thriller stories about murders and people who die in violent ways. If you found such things, you'd feel uncomfortable and think something was wrong. The same happens with digital communication. Discussing your school grades while your friend is talking about their dates might not be appropriate. The first topic requires a formal and factual tone, while the second is based on an emotional and informal one. Whenever you want to convey a clear message, make sure to consider the people you're talking to, where you are, and the main topic of discussion. I'm pretty sure that if you found yourself at a funeral, you wouldn't laugh all the time. Well, the same is valid online.

How Tone and Context Often Get Lost

In real life, tone and context are so obvious that we take them for granted. Most times, we manage to use the right tone and adapt our message to the context. What about online? Digital communication is more complicated than face-to-face because all those elements that help us understand a message (tone of voice, facial expressions, eye contact, gestures, etc.) are missing. Therefore, it's more likely that the person you communicate with doesn't understand what you mean and want. Moreover, having meaningful conversations is more difficult, as you don't feel like writing every single detail to further explain your point of view, or you don't want to send a 10-minute audio recording. Therefore, you're more likely to synthesize concepts or avoid discussing delicate topics. As boring as it might seem, paying attention to properly spell your words is fundamental to getting the message across. You should check grammar and punctuation and try as much as you can to write complete sentences and avoid abbreviations. This way, the person who receives the message will be more likely to understand it.

Imagine having a discussion with your partner on WhatsApp and writing something like, "I'm sorry, I love you." You might take for granted the fact that you wanted to say you're sorry for what you did and you love them. However, they might understand you're so angry at them that you're sorry you love them. Misunderstandings occur even more often when people feel angry or sad and interpret texts through their emotions. When reading your message, your partner might get even angrier, and the argument might go on longer than it should. Instead, if you write something like, "I'm sorry, I love you," you'll send a clearer message and avoid useless discussions. If you said the same thing in person, your partner would have understood your message thanks to non-verbal cues like your tone of voice. If you sound angry, then you probably mean you're sorry you love them. If you have a low tone of voice, look them in the eye, and your facial expression shows regret, then they understand that you're sorry and you want to make things right because you love them.

Another example that shows how tone and context are essential but get lost in texts is the word "Okay." We use it so often that we give it many different meanings. "Okay" could mean that we're fine, we want to end a conversation, or we want the other person to think they're right when we actually don't agree with them. Sometimes, we write "okay" and just hope the receiver understands that we're not really okay and need to discuss a specific topic further. Context and tone often get lost when people flirt online. Have you ever written a message to someone you wanted to date and realized your words might be misinterpreted only when you had already sent it? Well, it happens more often than you might believe. Maybe you're in a rush and send a message without checking it, then reopen it and notice what you wrote. You feel ashamed, but there's nothing you can do about it (except deleting it if the receiver hasn't read it yet). As you can see, tone and context often get lost and can cause many troubles in building and maintaining relationships.

THE DANGERS OF MISINTERPRETATION AND MISUNDERSTANDING

What Is a Misunderstanding of a Text

One of the most common problems in all types of communication is misunderstanding. Have you ever felt alone and sad because you thought nobody understood you? Well, you're not the only one, but there's a solution to your problem. Have you ever said or has someone ever told you something like, "I'm sorry if you were offended by what I said," or "I'm sorry you took it the wrong way?" That's usually how people respond when a misunderstanding occurs: They believe the reason behind such an issue consists of the listener's inability to understand their words. But is it really like that? If you know what "misunderstanding" means, you know the answer is negative. A misunderstanding happens when the speaker tries to convey a message to the listener, but what they want to express differs from what the other person thinks they want to express. In other words, the speaker's message doesn't correspond to what the listener understands. This means that both the speaker and listener are responsible for the unsuccessful communication. In fact, there are two types of misunderstandings: the speaker isn't aware that their message hasn't been understood, and the listener doesn't realize they haven't understood the message.

So, why do misunderstandings occur? The reasons are numerous. On the speaker's side, they might not have a clear idea in their mind, so they struggle to express it. They might know what they want to say but still find it difficult to properly communicate, or they might decide to omit some of their thoughts. In real life, the speaker might feel overwhelmed, angry, or simply want to vent, so they don't manage to process all their thoughts while they appear in their minds. Therefore, they might say things that differ from what they truly want to say, and the listener might easily misunderstand their words. It mainly occurs when the relationship is fresh, and you don't know each other. For example, you might vent with one of your new classmates about your parents, and they might give you some advice or answer in a way that doesn't corre-spond to reality because they don't know you or your family. If you know what you want to say but can't express it, you might not know or use the proper words to make others understand. If you're not used to explaining how you feel, you might struggle to do it. Finally, you might decide to omit essential information, as many of us do every day when we want to be polite, we're too proud to say certain things, or we fear others will use our ideas to manipulate us. For example, your new date might ask you something like, "I love Sci-Fi movies, do you?" and you might reply, "Well, I like Star Wars." You might not want to disappoint them or be rude and tell them you only like Star Wars but can't stand all other Sci-Fi movies. As you omitted some information, your partner might believe you like them and ask you to go to the cinema together every time a new Sci-Fi movie comes out.

What happens on the listener's side? Misunderstandings happen when the listener can't understand what the speaker says for cultural reasons and biases. For instance, you might talk about feminism and immigration with your friends, but they might misunderstand your words based on the meanings they associate with them. You might give the word "feminism" a positive connotation and think that it's good, while your friends might give it a negative. Misunderstandings also happen because of false beliefs, lack of experience, or a narrow worldview. Your parents might misunderstand your words when you talk about social media because they come from a different generation when technology wasn't as advanced as now. They might also lack the necessary experience to understand how technology works and the pros and cons of TikTok, Instagram, etc.

Impacts

As you probably found out on your own, misunderstandings can have a negative impact on your relationships in various ways. Simple misunderstandings can provoke conflicts, as we discussed in the previous section. Saying to your partner you need some time for yourself might make them believe you don't enjoy spending time with them. They might feel sad and scared because they believe you're going to dump them, and you might feel frustrated and disappointed because they don't understand what you mean. You might end up arguing for hours when you could have just explained yourself and asked them why they believe you don't love them anymore. If conflicts keep arising because of misunderstandings, trust issues might arise. Imagine texting your friend and fearing they won't understand what you mean. Your fear comes true, and they misinterpret your words. If such situations keep happening, you might feel insecure every time you want to text them. In other words, your relationship will suffer due to repeated misunderstandings. But misunderstandings also have negative impacts on our mental well-being. In fact, they cause confusion and frustration, and sometimes, they can even lead to stress and anxiety. If you put a lot of effort into interpreting the other person's messages, but most times you don't understand them, you might feel negative emotions. You might believe you're not clever enough to interpret a simple message, or you might feel frustrated. In general, misunderstandings are extremely time-wasting and can strain relationships.

What to Do About It

How can we avoid misunderstandings? No matter if you're the speaker or the listener—the following tips will help you. First of all, you must carefully listen to what the others say. During conversations, our minds tend to roam and focus on other aspects, like people around us, what we're going to eat for dinner, or the next picture we're going to share on Instagram. As hard as it might look, try to concentrate on the speaker's words and ask clarifying questions if you think you didn't grasp what they mean.

Moreover, you must keep in mind that what you hear is often different from what others say. Because of our fears, we tend to perceive facts differently from reality. For example, you might tell your partner you need some time for yourself, or you want to go out with your friends more often. If they suffer from fear of abandonment, they might understand you don't like spending time with them. If such situations occur, don't escalate but ask them the reasons behind their words to understand what made them think that way.

Other common mistakes that cause misunderstandings are not believing the speaker's words, making assumptions, and attacking the other person. If listening is hard, believing the speaker is even more difficult. Whenever you argue with someone, avoid thinking that you know what's going on in their heads and they're not being sincere with you. Listen to them, believe in their words, and just drop it. We all make assumptions based on past experiences and think we can predict what the other person will say and do. In reality, we can't. Instead of convincing yourself that you already know how a conversation will go, talk to the other person kindly and compassionately and ask them questions to avoid misunderstandings. Finally, people easily misunderstand sentences like, "You're always late" or "You never listen to me." Such words are usually considered a direct attack and make the other person react defensively. They close themselves off and stop talking, or they attack in response. That's how a simple misunderstanding generates an endless argument. To avoid such situations, just be kind to them and use "I" sentences where you express how you feel first, like "I feel frustrated when you arrive late and don't even text me to notify me."

STRATEGIES FOR RECOVERING LOST MESSENGERS

How to Read Between the Lines

We looked at some tips to avoid misunderstandings in the previous section. Now, let's discover some strategies to recover the lost messengers in texts: Tone and context. The first strategy we'll look at concerns reading between the lines. You might have found yourself in a situation when you didn't have many clues to understand what another person meant and didn't know what to do. As happens to all of us, I guess you really wanted to be able to read between the lines. Well, you can. First, you must always assume good intentions. When someone texts you, they might send words without emojis, exclamation points, etc. Therefore, you might struggle to read between the lines. Unless they explicitly tell you they feel angry or sad, don't assume it. Think positive and convince yourself the other person's fine and happy to talk with you.

Second, you must become aware of common unconscious biases. For example, males and females tend to express and understand emotions differently. A researcher conducted a study with coding teams that had to interpret texts (Davis, 2016). Each coding team had to read texts and decide which emotion the person who sent them was feeling. They read a message saying, "My wife forgot about our 10th anniversary." Male members of the coding team thought that the message expressed anger, while female members believed it expressed sadness. Whenever you receive a message from someone (especially if you know them), consider their characteristics and how they might differ from you. Thirdly, you must carefully read each word to explore its emotional undertone. Words like happiness, wonderful, love, excitement, etc., usually express positive feelings. Conversely, words like hard, difficult, hate, sadness, work, etc., represent negative emotions. Attach an emotional undertone to every word you read to understand how the sender of the message is feeling. If you think the message is contradictory, ask for clarification.

Picking up Patterns

When writing texts, we all follow specific patterns or habits. We tend to use the same words or emojis to express a thought or emotion and believe others will immediately understand what we mean. Well, some patterns and habits are efficient while others aren't. Did you know that adding a period at the end of a message makes you look insincere? That's what research found out (Cutolo, 2023). If you're used to texting something like "Okay." or "Yup.", I suggest you delete the period and send the message without it. Alternatively, you can replace the period with an exclamation mark. Emojis can help the receiver understand how you feel, but not if you overuse them. If you send a message with five words and ten emojis, then it's more likely that the receiver will misunderstand your words. Another annoying habit is waiting for days to answer a message. We all have that one friend who never looks at their phone or opens all the messages when they're busy and forgets to answer them. If you're that friend, I suggest you try to adjust your behavior and show other people you think about them more often than once every two or three days.

To make others understand you care about them and dedicate a few seconds of your life to answer them, you must also avoid shortening all letters or sending one-letter messages like "k." Most people perceive it as rude and believe you don't even have a few more seconds to add an "o" in front of the "k." Another annoying habit is to send one syllable per text and add an exclamation or question mark in another text. This way, the receiver will hear their phone beeping many times and will probably feel frustrated. Moreover, your message is clearer if you write everything you have to say in just one text. One thing we should all avoid is to apologize via text. Saying sorry on WhatsApp or in person is completely different. If you had to do it once or someone did it to you, you know what I mean. When you send a text saying, "I'm sorry," you don't look regretful, and it seems you want to avoid the conversation and forget about your mistake as soon as you can. The above are just examples of common patterns we all engage in. To make sure your messages are understood, you can reflect on your habits and change the ones that might cause misunderstandings.

Inferring Emotions

To recover the lost messengers of tone and context, you can also learn to infer emotions from texts. Before doing it, you must let go of all your assumptions and biases and accept that you can't know how a person feels—even if they're your best friend, parent, or partner. Taking a high grade at school can provoke different emotional reactions depending on a person's characteristics and background. You might feel satisfied because you got a B on your math exam, while your best friend might be upset. The reasons behind such different emotions can be that your parents are used to telling you that you mustn't get all A's to be a good student, while your best friend's parents are stricter. After letting go of your assumptions, you can infer emotions by working on your personal theory of emotions and increasing your knowledge. Over the decades, psychologists have developed various theories to explain where emotions come from and what they mean. Even if you're not a psychologist, you can do the same for yourself. Try to reflect on how you perceive emotions and what you think they mean. For example, you can ask yourself something like, *Whenever I feel angry, do other emotions arise, or is it the only feeling I get?* Once you understand your emotions, you can properly express them so that people understand you more easily. You can also use your personal theory to understand others' feelings and compare them with yours. In general, the best way to understand what people mean in their messages is to ask them questions to clarify their ideas. Even if you're 99% sure your friend is upset, ask them how they feel to find out if you're right or not—don't just assume you're right.

CASE STUDIES: UNDERSTANDING TONE IN DIGITAL CONVERSATION

Using tone in digital communication is not impossible. You can make people understand what you mean in various ways. The most popular ones are abbreviations like LOL (Laughing Out Loud) or OJ (Only Joking), which send a clear message to the receiver. Imagine sending to your best friend two versions of the same message, one that says, "You're so late I'm going to head home," and the other that says, "You're so late I'm going to head home OJ." In the first case, your friend might read the message and think they're not going to find you at the place you decided to meet. Therefore, confusion and misunderstandings might arise. In the second case, your friend immediately understands you're joking and notifies you they're going to arrive soon. Another common way in which you can transmit tone is through emojis. Using too much might distract the receiver and blur your message, but using the right amount can be helpful. In general, adding an emoji at the end of the text is enough to get your point across.

The tone of voice is so essential that iconic brands dedicate a lot of time to refining it. To make customers understand their point, they pay a lot of attention to the words and images they use. For example, Starbucks always tries to convey both a functional and expressive tone of voice. A functional tone indicates that the brand gives importance to clear language. In fact, user experience, like ordering, is always easy to navigate. An expressive tone of voice helps customers get the idea that Starbucks is fresh, relevant, and interesting. Is it how you perceive the brand? If so, then their tone of voice clearly expresses their message (Gilbert, 2022). If it chose a different tone, you would probably think about it differently.

DIY

Are you good at expressing and understanding tone of voice and context? Choose a short story or passage and replace key emotional words with emojis. Share the emoji version with a friend and ask them to interpret the emotions and context. Compare their interpretation to your original intention. Is their interpretation different

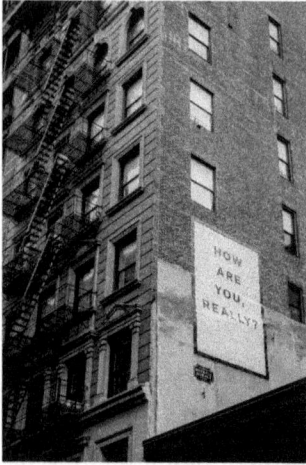

from yours? If so, how does it make you feel? Did you discuss it with your friends, too, to see what they thought about it?

In this chapter, we learned everything we needed about tone and context. We discovered that, most times, tone and context get lost in messages, but we can recover them in various ways. First, we must avoid misunderstandings by eliminating some common mistakes, like focusing on our assumptions and biases and using them to interpret others' words. But we can recover tone and context also by learning to read between the lines, identifying common habits that provoke misunderstandings, and inferring emotions from texts. In this chapter, we also briefly introduced emojis and how we can use them to properly express our emotions. In Chapter 3, we'll dive deep into the topic of emojis, their pros and cons, and how we can limit their use to improve our digital communication.

3

BEYOND EMOJIS - THE POWER OF WORDS

66 *Communication works for those who work at it.*

— JOHN POWELL

B y now, we all use emojis to express how we feel in texts, but are they really helpful? Do they help others understand our emotions? In this chapter, we'll discover that it's not always as easy as we think. We'll find out the limitations of emojis and in which cases they can be effective. We'll also look at alternative strategies we can use to express our emotions, such as building an in-depth vocabulary and using descriptive language. Finally, we'll find useful, practical exercises to improve the way we communicate through texts.

EMOJIS AND THEIR LIMITATIONS

What Emojis Cannot Convey

A few years ago, I had an interesting conversation with one of my friends. At that time, I used to use the emoji "XD" in many of my messages. I was sure about its meaning, so I used it when I thought it was appropriate. But then, my friend asked me, "Why do you keep using that emoji? It seems like you always feel sad or devastated." I was so surprised by their question that I asked them why they thought that. They replied, "You see, the 'X' means that your eyes are closed like when you're crying while the 'D' represents your mouth completely open as if you're shouting." I didn't know what to say because I always gave another meaning to that emoji; I thought it indicated awkwardness but in a funny way, as sometimes you see in

Japanese anime. My friend's explanation made me think a lot and decide I wouldn't use the "XD" emoji anymore to avoid people believing I was sad. How many times do we send emojis, attaching them with a certain meaning, while others interpret them differently? I guess it happens more often than we can imagine.

Do you know where the word "emoji" comes from? It's composed of two Japanese terms: "e" stands for "picture" and "moji" for "character" or "letter" (Holland, 2017). Although you might believe they're universal and anyone interprets them in the same way, that's not completely true. As insignificant as it might look, different platforms or new versions of the same apps translate and depict emojis differently. For example, if you send an emoji to your best friend on your iPhone, they might see it differently on their Android. In new versions of the iPhone, emojis change compared to older versions. In 2016, a survey discovered that the famous emoji "grinning face with smiling eyes" meant "blissfully happy" for people with an Android and "ready to fight" for those who had an iPhone (Levine, 2019).

Moreover, the same emoji can have various meanings in different contexts. The popular "folded hands" emoji represents a high-five, a prayer, and thanks at the same time. Can you imagine how many misunderstandings it can create? If that's not enough, each emoji can have a different meaning depending on your social group or generation. You can test your parents by asking them how they would interpret a particular emoji. Their answers might surprise you. Emojis have become so essential in our everyday conversations that even international courts have become more and more interested in them. In fact, many people use them to prove their point in legal cases. In the last decades, U.S. courts have addressed emojis in business cases that concern issues of sexual harassment, employment discrimination, and breach of contracts (Levine, 2019). Just think about how ambiguous the winking face is or the fact that you can change the skin color of your emoji. They can reasonably provoke misunderstandings.

The main problem with emojis is that people use them to convey emotions. However, emotions are complicated and already difficult to express in words. People already struggle to understand how others feel when they have physical cues like body language, facial expressions, and so on. Understanding emotions through little faces on the screen looks almost impossible.

How to Effectively Use Emojis

You might ask yourself, "*Does this mean I shouldn't use emojis anymore because they just cause problems?*" Well, it doesn't. We can all use emojis effectively to enhance the meaning of our texts and help others understand how we feel. The general rule of thumb is to avoid all emojis that might have an ambiguous meaning, especially those that represent vegetables and other food. Stick to the classics: a heart, a smiley face, or a thumbs-up. Keep in mind that depending on people's cultures and backgrounds, they can give a different meaning to the same emoji, so you must make sure you send simple ones. Another tip to effectively use emojis consists of putting them at the end of your sentence and using one or two for each text. When you're not sure about the meaning of an emoji, you can also consult the almighty Emojipedia. If you've never heard of it, I suggest you look at it. You can find the names and explanations of all emojis, emojis that might appear in your smartphone in the future, and how they're depicted on various devices and platforms.

However, the fact that you look at Emojipedia doesn't mean everyone does it, so others can still misunderstand your emojis or give them different meanings. If you want to effectively use emojis, you should use them just to enhance your message and not replace it. Remember to always write what you want to say in words, and if you want to clarify a concept, add an emoji or two. Finally, make sure the emojis you choose to match the text you write. For example, if you want to show enthusiasm to your best friend who asked you if you feel like going to a party on Saturday night, you can text them, "Let's go," and add the fist emoji at the end to make them understand you're psyched to go. Adding emojis before words under-mines their meaning and value, while inserting one that doesn't match your text might confuse others. Imagine texting your friend something like, "Let's go," and adding a sleepy face—they might misunderstand what you mean.

BUILDING A VOCABULARY

Strategies for Expanding Your Vocabulary

The more words you know, the easier you express how you feel and what you think. Building a strong vocabulary is essential to avoid misunderstandings and clarify your thoughts because it gives you the opportunity to use different words to express various ideas and emotions. Just think about all the times you use the words "sad" or "happy" to define how you feel. Do they really represent your emotions, or are they simplifications? Instead of saying you feel happy, wouldn't you prefer being more precise and using words like enthusiastic, delighted, excited, energetic, or thrilled? Wouldn't you want to replace the word "sad" with more specific definitions, like down, uncomfortable, blue, upset, or distressed? You'll get your message across more easily if you replace generic words with specific ones that make others understand what you have inside. A strong vocabulary doesn't only allow you to improve your relationships and boost your communication skills, but it also helps you achieve better results at school and have a deep understanding of the world around you. As you can see, a strong vocabulary can improve your life in various ways.

How can you build your vocabulary? You can use numerous strategies and just have to choose the ones you find more interesting and funnier. If you're into studying humanistic subjects, you can follow some Greek or Latin classes. As boring as they might look, they can boost your vocabulary and help you understand what a word means even if you've never seen or heard it before. Whenever you want to learn a new concept, make sure to check how you can express it formally and informally. For example, you can use the expression "get your foot in the door" when you talk with your loved ones and say "expand your opportunities" in a formal context. Adjusting your language and vocabulary depending on the people around you is essential to get the message across and avoid misunderstandings. After learning new words, you can take vocabulary tests to help you retain them and check your progress.

You can invent your tests or look at them online. Communication and writing skills go hand in hand. That's why the more you improve your vocabulary, the more people will understand your spoken and written words. Therefore, you must take writing classes. You can take them online or just dedicate a few minutes of your day to keep a journal. You can incorporate this strategy with the previous one by writing down how your day was using the words you learned. For example, if you found out that "gargantuan" means "very large," you can use that word to describe something you noticed during the day. This way, you'll remember new words more easily.

Another effective strategy to expand your vocabulary is to look for synonyms, antonyms, and words with similar meanings. For this purpose, I recommend you use the online dictionary Thesaurus, where you can also find funny activities and games linked with words. When you learn that not all synonyms have exactly the same meaning and you can't replace them as if they were the same, you'll pay more attention to the words you use. Moreover, remember to always edit what you write—no matter the context. Whenever you send a text to your best friend, an email to your teachers, or a cover letter for a job opportunity, read it again and again before sending it.

Check your spelling and grammar and ask yourself if your message is clear or if you used some ambiguous words. Last but not least, the almighty strategy to improve your vocabulary consists of reading. The more you diversify your readings, the more words you learn. If you think reading is boring or you struggle to keep your focus for a long time, remember you don't have to read endless fiction novels. Just go to a bookstore and choose the book you find more interesting, even if it's only 30 pages long. You can choose among fiction, non-fiction, poems, short stories, and much more. Start small and, if you enjoy reading, gradually increase the complexity and length of the books you choose.

BEYOND EMOJIS | 55

The Emotion Wheel

Did you know that humans can experience more than 34,000 different emotions? Other estimates calculate we can feel "only" 27, but that's still a lot to process (Cooks-Campbell, 2022). Obviously, nobody will ever be able to recognize, understand, and properly label all such emotions, but we can still give it a try and expand our knowledge. If you've never heard of the emotion wheel, you're probably wondering what it looks like: It's like a colored Ferris wheel that contains all emotions based on their intensity. It's a graph composed of eight core emotions (joy, trust, surprise, anticipation, sadness, fear, anger, and disgust) and secondary ones. Psychologist Robert Plutchik invented the emotion wheel to simplify the infinite range of human feelings (Cooks-Campbell, 2022). Thanks to his emotion wheel, you can understand all the nuances emotions have. If someone tells you something like, "You must be sad that you got a low grade even if you studied a lot," you can reply, "I'm not sad. I'm just a bit disappointed." In other words, you'll be able to understand the intensity of each emotion and which one better represents your emotional state.

To understand the emotion wheel, you must first know how it looks. At the center of the wheel, there are the eight core emotions divided between uncomfortable and comfortable. Each core emotion is paired up with its opposite: sadness with joy, trust with disgust, anger with fear, and anticipation with surprise. Opposite emotions don't cancel each other but create a more intense interaction between them. For example, if you're suffering because you lost a loved person and meet someone who looks enthusiastic, you might feel confused and even more devastated than before. In other words, opposites don't attract each other. On the internet, you can find various versions of Plutchik's wheel, which are all valid, so you can choose the one that helps you visualize and understand emotions. Some are more colored, while others divide core emotions differently (for instance, you can find a wheel with just six core emotions). Choose the one that seems clearer to you.

Why would you want to use an emotion wheel? The essential reason is it boosts your self-awareness. Sometimes, emotions are straightforward, and you immediately understand how you feel. If someone offers you a gift, you correctly and rapidly label the emotion you feel as gratitude. However, classifying emotions is not always easy. You might feel contradictory feelings at the same time and feel confused. In such cases, the emotion wheel can come in handy and help you interpret how you feel. You can start by looking at the core emotions, which are easier to label and recognize, and then check the secondary emotions and reflect on the one that better suits your emotional state. An emotion wheel also helps you understand that you have control over your emotions. Thanks to it, you can trace back how you feel to its trigger or origin. In other words, you realize there's always an event, other emotion, or behavior that generates the emotion you feel. Imagine being sure that you feel over-whelmed. Therefore, you feel an uncomfortable emotion linked with fear. Consequently, you might ask yourself what makes you feel afraid and get to the roots of your problems.

After using the emotion wheel for some time, you'll also be able to respond and not react to emotions. When we react, we activate the fight-or-flight response that makes us face the problem or run away from it. It's an instinctive reaction to a threat. To take control of our emotions, we must overcome the fight-or-flight response and actively respond to the threat by becoming more aware of the nuances of our emotions. Whenever we have a feeling, we must check the emotion wheel and precisely label it. When you realize you feel overwhelmed, you become aware of the aspects of your life that make you feel like that. Conversely, when you feel generically sad, you might struggle to understand what goes wrong and change it.

The emotion wheel can improve your self-awareness and relationship with others because it helps you precisely label and recognize your emotions and understand others. It's an incredible and simple tool that can change your life.

USING DESCRIPTIVE LANGUAGE IN TEXT

How Descriptive Language Is Useful

Descriptive language is a language used to describe people, places, things, or situations. Descriptive language helps others understand your message and your intentions clearly. If you want to effectively communicate online, you can use vivid details, adjectives, adverbs, similes, and metaphors. Descriptive language is based on a lot of small details that paint a clear picture of a specific situation. Good writers use the five senses to help readers understand what's going on. For example, if a person is lying down on the grass looking at the sky, good writers describe their posture, body language, facial expression, and everything they perceive with their senses (what they hear, smell, taste, see, and touch). If you decide to keep a journal, as mentioned in the previous sections, you can use it to try your writing skills. In addition to writing what happens during the day using the words you learn, you can also practice descriptive language. When you start writing your diary, describe your school, how you got there, what your classroom and classmates look like, and so on.

Use your imagination, and feel free to write whatever you want. After all, nobody's going to read your journal unless you give them your permission. Even if you feel like you're not an expert writer or you're not good at writing, just give it a try and see how it goes. You don't have to use enigmatic or complex words, but you should use straightforward language you feel comfortable with. Just remember to add a few new words now and then to retain them better. Imagine you're the main character of your book series and must describe what you do. Put emphasis on all the small things you do daily—even brushing your teeth or having breakfast. Try to be as precise as possible and describe your life using all your five senses.

If you write about the route you take every day to go to school, ask yourself, *"What do I smell while going to school? Do I hear some particular noises? What do I see? Do I taste something? How do my feet feel while walking? Do I touch something like the car's steering wheel while driving or a handrail while climbing up the stairs?"* Think of all the details, even the most insignificant ones, and write them down with descriptive language. After practicing for a while, you can start using descriptive language when talking. This way, you'll stop saying things like "Can you pass me that thing over there?" or giving the wrong directions to people on the street. In other words, you'll learn to properly describe the world around and inside you.

EXERCISES FOR COMMUNICATION

Are you curious to see the effects of online communication and discover the power of words? Try the following activities alone or with your friends.

- **Spread gossip in your group of friends:**

Think about a situation that could lead all your friends to discuss it in private and not all together. Then, choose a friend you want to tell the gossip. For example, you can text them that one of your classmates has just been dumped, so it's single again after some time. Next, tell the same gossip to another friend in person. Try to track down the gossip told on the phone and the one in person and see what happens. Were there more misunderstandings online or offline? Did your initial gossip change? Was it modified more often by text or in person? How did you feel about gossiping on the phone or face-to-face? What can you take away from this activity?

- **The listener and the talker:**

Try this activity with one of your friends. As you might guess, one of you plays the role of the listener while the other plays the talker. The talker must think about a topic they would like to discuss without explicitly telling the most important element of their argument. Let's say your best friend plays the talker. They can decide to describe how their ideal holiday should look like or what they look for in a perfect holiday without saying a specific city or country. Your role as a listener is just to listen to their words. When your best friend has concluded their argument, you must summarize what they said and guess what the best holiday can be for them. You can propose cities or countries as you prefer. If you've been a good listener, you remember the main elements of your best friend's argument and can identify a city or country where they would enjoy spending their holidays. Once you finish the activity, you can switch roles.

- **The memory test:**

Thanks to it, you retain new concepts more easily. Therefore, you learn more words in less time. You can try this activity alone or with other people. If you do it by yourself, I suggest you record some words in advance and then listen to them when you want to try the exercise. If you do it with other people, tell them you're going to read some words from a list, and they must listen carefully. They can't write down what they hear, and you're not going to repeat the list. Slowly say the words out loud, pausing between each one. Here's a list you can use: dream, mattress, tired, sleep, night, snooze, insomnia, sleep, alarm, pillow, blanket, nap, sleep. I suggest you start practicing the activity with words you already know so that you get used to it. Once you master the memory test, you can try it with complicated new concepts you want to learn. After saying all the words, let some time pass by distracting others or yourself. Listen to some music, do your homework, clean your bedroom, or just take a walk. Let your mind roam and don't try to remember the words. After a few minutes, take a piece of paper and a pencil and write down all the words you recall. Then, check them with the original list. You'll probably notice you don't remember many words. That's because carefully listening and remembering aren't easy tasks. But if you keep practicing, you'll become good at them.

- **Manage your anger:**

Learning to understand and express your emotions is essential to properly communicate how you feel and what you think, especially when texting. One of the emotions we all struggle to express is anger. Some people try to deny or avoid it, while others become so aggressive that they make people feel defensive. To boost communication skills, you must learn to recognize and manage anger. You can do this activity by yourself or with your family members, friends, and partner. First, think about a time you were upset and how it made you feel. Consider your thoughts and your body: What were you thinking? How were your muscles, heart rate, and hands? If you do the exercise with someone else, ask others how they perceive you when you feel upset to understand the difference between your self-image and how others see you. Then, ask yourself the same questions, but think about a time you felt particularly relaxed and had a good time. Finally, consider the cues that trigger your anger and what you can do to properly manage the emotion.

The above activities are just examples that show you how you can work on your communication and listening skills, memory, and emotions. If you try such exercises and find them entertaining and helpful, you can search online for more.

DIY

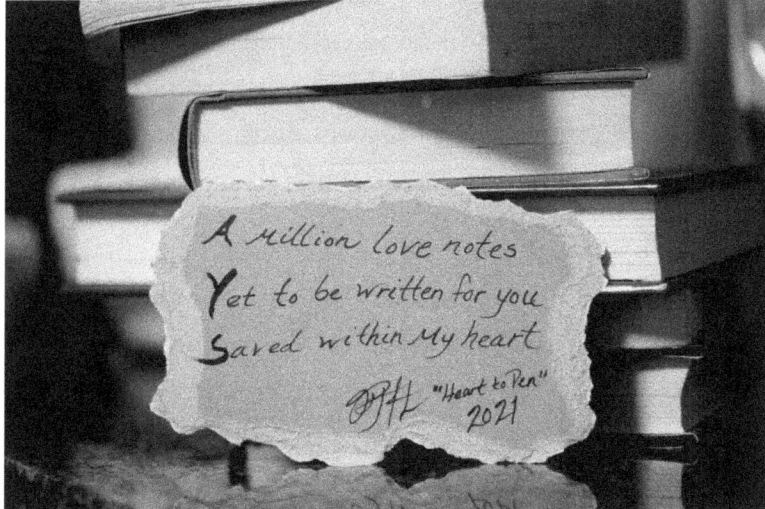

Do you know what a haiku is? It's a brief Japanese poetic form that is composed of just three lines. The first line contains five syllables, the second seven, and the third five. You will find an example of what a haiku looks like in the picture above. To practice everything you learned in this chapter, you can write your own haiku. First, select an emotion you've recently experienced. Second, write your haiku using the descriptive language you previously learned. Describe the emotion using as many details as you can without directly mentioning it. For example, if you choose to write about frustration, you can use all the words you want except "frustration," "frustrated," or similar. Finally, share your haiku with a friend and see if they can identify the emotion you portrayed. If so, congratulations! You've managed to effectively use descriptive language and know how to properly express your emotions by text. If not, you can retry the activity all the times you want. Keep in mind that you mustn't be a poet or an excellent writer to write your haiku, and you mustn't even be precise in respecting the correct number of syllables. You must have fun while trying the activity.

In this chapter, we discovered the origins of emojis and how they have pros and cons. On one hand, they can help us enhance our message and convey it more clearly. On the other hand, they can be confusing because not all of us attach the same meaning and emotion to them. Next, we learned that having a strong vocabulary is essential to make others understand how we feel and what we think, especially when we text. Some strategies to expand our vocabulary include reading a lot and learning new words every day. The emotion wheel is another useful tool that allows us to recognize, understand, label, and properly express how we feel. In the last two sections, we also looked at entertaining activities we can try by ourselves or with our loved ones to boost our communication and listening skills. In Chapter 4, we'll dive deep into the topic of emotions and discuss a fundamental element that helps us understand our emotions and those of others: Empathy.

4

EMPATHETIC DIGITAL
COMMUNICATION

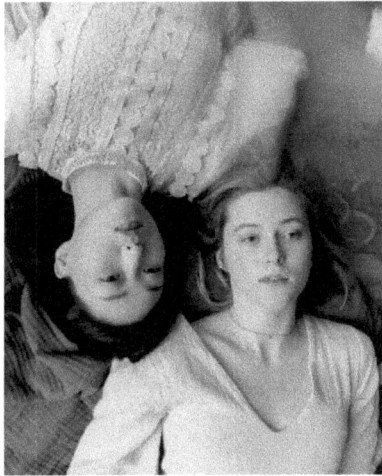

" *Constantly talking isn't necessarily commu-nicating.*

— CHARLIE KAUFMAN

The fourth strategy we'll look at in this chapter consists of mastering the art of empathy. Have you ever been hurt by someone, online or offline? Maybe they sent you a rude comment on TikTok and made you feel misunderstood and attacked. Or maybe you really needed help from someone, but they refused with a pathetic excuse. In both cases, the reason why they hurt you is they lack empathy. If all humans weren't empathetic, we would live in a world where everyone thinks for themselves. In the long run, we would live in a world without people, as we all need to feel connected with and supported by others. Although empathy is becoming more and more underrated, it's essential to survive and build strong relationships. In the next sections of this chapter, we'll discover what empathy is, its importance, and how to recognize it in others. Next, we'll learn useful and straightforward techniques to express empathy online and recognize emotional cues in texts. Finally, we'll look at some case studies linked with empathy and a practical activity that shows us how empathy works in real life.

EMPATHY

What It Is

You might have heard the word "empathy" many times, but do you know what it means? It's the ability to understand, recognize, label, and express your emotions. But it's

BEYOND EMOJIS | 69

also much more than that, as it's also the ability to understand and recognize others' emotions. Defining "empathy" is no easy task because it involves various elements. First, empathy is an essential factor that composes our emotional intelligence. If your level of emotional intelligence is high, it means that you can be very empathetic toward others. You can't be emotionally intelligent without being empathetic.

A common misunderstanding that makes defining empathy even harder is the confusion between that concept and sympathy. If you feel sympathetic, you feel *for* someone. In other words, you understand how they feel and show it to them. If you feel empathetic, you feel *with* them. It looks as if you can enter their mind and feel exactly the same way they feel. You not only understand their emotions but feel them inside you. You identify yourself with their situation and understand what they're going through. What distinguishes empathy from sympathy is that you need to use a lot of imagination to express the former. In fact, you don't need to go through the same circumstances that other people are facing to understand how they feel and feel the same. Thanks to your imagination, you can precisely infer how they're doing (*Empathy*, 2019).

However, empathy also has a downside. Putting yourself in others' shoes fosters cooperation and builds relationships, but it can also have a negative effect on you. If you just keep empathizing and helping others, you might end up forgetting about your needs or becoming vulnerable to people who take advantage of your kindness and openness. Therefore, we must all be careful and find the perfect balance: We mustn't be too empathetic or too little. If you feel like you don't need or don't want to become more empathetic because you don't want to be vulnerable in front of others, keep in mind that empathy has various benefits. A lot of research has shown how it boosts relationships and our overall well-being throughout our lives (What Is Empathy?, 2011). Being empathetic means cooperating with others, building friendships, and effectively making moral decisions. If an empathetic person witnesses someone being bullied, they immediately act to help them. If you want to live a happier life, you must learn to become more empathetic.

Signs of an Empathetic Person

Now, you know what empathy means, but are you able to recognize an empathetic person when you meet them? Let's look at some typical signs of someone who feels and expresses empathy. If you're an empathetic person, your main characteristic is that you're a good listener. People are naturally drawn toward you because they know they can tell you whatever they want, and you'll carefully listen to every single word they say. You'll not only listen to them, but you'll also try to understand their point of view and avoid judging them. No matter what they tell you— you'll always do your best to put yourself in their shoes and understand the reasons behind their words and behavior. As you can see, such a quality can boost your relationships and help you deeply connect with others. If people know you never judge them, even if they do something wrong, they'll be more likely to become your friends and trust you.

Imagine your best friend coming to you to cry about the fact that their partner dumped them. If you're empathetic, you try to comfort them in all ways, you let them talk and vent using all the time they need, and you avoid giving them advice or thinking about other things. You just focus on the conversation with them, and all your attention is drawn toward their words. You never interrupt them, change the subject, or start talking about yourself. If you're empathetic, your best friend will feel understood, taken care of, and relaxed. They know they'll always have a shoulder to cry on when they need it.

But empathy is much more than that. It also involves picking up on non-verbal cues, feeling your and others' emotions intensely, offering support, and being adaptable. When people talk to you, you not only listen to their words but also look at their posture, facial expression, eyes, and so on. You check if their words match their body language and look for cues on their intentions. For these reasons, you're also more likely to understand when someone lies because you feel like something's off with what they say. Maybe their words don't match previous conversations, or their body language doesn't correspond to what they're saying. As much as you're good at talking with people, you might also feel drained by social situations. If you're empathetic, you tend to avoid small talk because you find it useless and feel overwhelmed by all the emotions people around you are feeling. Talking to others might make you feel anxious, exhausted, or even depressed, depending on how they feel. Imagine yourself being a sponge: You absorb all the emotions around you. As you might guess, spending a night out chatting with people might make you feel devastated.

How Empathy Fosters Connections

You might ask yourself, "*How is empathy going to boost the connections I already have and new ones?*" Well, there are various ways. First, you must know the different styles of empathy: Affective, cognitive, and somatic. Affective empathy is strictly connected with emotions. Therefore, you manage to feel how others feel and identify with their emotions. Cognitive empathy concerns the ability to think about what others are thinking. In other words, you understand people's mental states and the way they perceive the world. Somatic empathy refers to physical reactions to others' emotions. For example, an empathetic person who interacts with someone who feels embarrassed might start blushing on their behalf. As you might guess, being empathetic fosters deep connections. When you feel empathetic and identify with other's emotions and thoughts, you feel like you're truly connected to them and can understand them on a deeper level. At the same time, those who interact with empathetic people feel understood in ways they didn't know were possible. Consequently, they feel profoundly connected. However, research has found some differences between males and females (Reid, 2023). Females usually report feeling sad when others are suffering more often than males. Studies involving Functional Magnetic Resonance Imaging (fMRI) confirmed that female brains are more receptive to feeling others' pain. Thanks to empathy, you can increase your emotional intelligence, improve your communication online and offline, build deeper connections, and increase your compassion.

TECHNIQUES FOR EMPATHY

Expressing Empathy Over Text

Expressing empathy in person is already pretty hard. Has someone ever told you something terrible that happened to them, and you didn't know how to answer? You might have opted for something like, "Look at the bright side," "This too shall pass," or "Something better is around the corner." These are classic responses we all use when we don't know how to reply, but we can do much better than that—both online and offline. Whenever someone opens up with you, you can express empathy in various ways. You can make others feel understood, heard, and validated by using some compassionate statements like, "I'm here for you," "I'm sorry you're going through this," or "That sounds really challenging." This way, others know that you're present and ready to help whenever they need something. They also get the idea that you're happy to listen to their troubles and worries.

To show empathy, you must also use open-ended questions. If you ask closed-ended questions, the other person can only reply "Yes" or "No." Therefore, you don't allow the conversation to go deeper and analyze the situation. If you want to ask your best friend how they're doing, you could ask them, "How are you?" instead of "Are you okay?" In the first case, they'll feel encouraged to tell more about their emotions. Once someone has opened up with you in person or through text, you can also use follow-up questions to see if the situation has improved. For example, you can send another message to your best friend asking them something like, "How do you feel today?"

If you find yourself in a difficult situation and don't know what to say, you can simply be honest. Sometimes, it's better to say nothing than to use the conventional and overrated answers we saw above. You can say something like, "Wow, I really don't know what to say," or "I can't imagine what you must be going through." Alternatively, you can show gratitude for the fact that the other person opened up to you. For instance, you can use sentences like, "I'm glad you opened up with me. That means a lot",

"Thank you for sharing," or "It must be hard to talk about it, thanks for trusting me."

During the conversation, you can also show interest by asking more questions, investigating how they feel, or repeating their sentences to make sure you correctly understood what they told you. Moreover, remember to always be encouraging and supportive. Don't hesitate to tell them they're brave, you love them, they matter to you, or you're proud of them. You can also offer help by asking them if they need something in particular or making a kind gesture.

In general, there's no specific script on how to show empathy to others. What you must keep in mind is that actions are better than words. In addition to expressing your gratitude, showing interest, and so on, you must also carefully listen to what they want to say and do your best to make them feel better.

Showing Someone You Understand Over Text

How can you show someone you understand what they're going through over text? As always, the answer is listening. Do you think about what you can say next when you talk to someone? Do you focus more on your point of view than on the others'? Think about a recent conversation you had with your parents, friends, or partner. Did you truly listen to them or just think about the best advice to give them or how you could introduce a different argument you wanted to discuss? If so, you don't need to feel ashamed. We all mind our own businesses from time to time and forget how important it is to listen to others. To show you comprehend, you must focus on understanding before focusing on being understood. Only in this way can you deepen your connections with others and increase your probability of being heard.

You might believe that showing you understand is easy, as you just have to say something like, "I understand." In most cases, that's not enough: People need something more to be 100% sure you understand their point of view. Therefore, you must explicitly say what you understand and ask if you correctly interpreted their words. You don't have to agree with the other person to show you understand. You can have different ideas and still accept their point of view.

The secret behind showing you understand others is to be completely honest with them. People often realize when others are lying or omitting some information, although unconsciously. In the long term, if you're insincere, others will notice it and you'll risk ruining your relationships. Therefore, being sincere is the best way to maintain your connections and show you understand your loved ones. If you don't, just say it and ask for clarifications, like you already learned.

Moreover, showing you understand also means you face difficult conversations with sensitivity and know how to balance honesty and politeness. You must be careful and think about when is the appropriate time to tell the truth and when is the appropriate time to just support others and avoid being considered rude. Whenever you want to show you understand your loved ones, take a few seconds to reflect on what you can say. Do you think you should encourage them and show sensitivity, or do you think they should know the naked truth? You should also consider their personality and how they could react in both situations to choose the best course of action.

EMOTIONAL CUES

Recognizing Them

Now that you know how to show empathy over text, you must understand how to recognize and respond to emotional cues. If your best friend expressly writes they feel angry, disappointed, or happy, it's easy to understand their emotions. But what happens when they just discuss a topic, and you have to associate the most appropriate emotion with it? As happens to all of us, you might struggle to read the emotional cues written between the lines. The most effective way of understanding how others feel over texts is to look at punctuation marks, spelling, capitalization, spacing, and emojis. If your best friend writes something like, "I can't go out next Saturday because I'm going on a trip with my family," the meaning of their words can change depending on the emoji they attach at the end. If they add a sad face, it means they don't feel like going on a trip with their family, while if they add a happy emoji, then they want to. Another effective way of recognizing emotional cues consists of looking at how others write the words.

For example, they might make intentional misspellings or space letters playfully. Just think about the two following messages: "Text me when you can" and "Text me ASAP." Do they convey two different meanings? I guess so, as the second message might make you feel the urge to reply as soon as possible. In some cases, the way letters are spaced can even make you hear them inside your head. Have you ever read a text in your mind as if you were yelling because someone sent you a message in caps lock? If so, it means you unconsciously attached a specific meaning to the words, so you recognized the emotional cues the sender wanted to convey.

Punctuation marks can also help you understand how your loved ones feel. If they send you many question marks followed by exclamation points, it probably indicates a feeling of surprise, excitement, or curiosity, depending on the specific context. In any case, question marks and exclamation points convey a positive emotion. Conversely, periods are perceived negatively, as we already discovered in Chapter 2. If you want to convey negative emotions, like harshness or flatness, you might want to add a period at the end of your sentences. This is also considered an effective way of ending a conversation. You must always keep in mind that texts won't completely replace a phone call or even a face-to-face meeting where you can look at non-verbal cues. No matter how hard you try to understand emotional cues over text—you'll always struggle more than in person to get an idea of how others feel.

How to Respond to Them

Once you understand how others feel, what can you do to respond to them? You can use the easy mnemonic "NURSE," which stands for Naming, Understanding, Respecting, Supporting, and Exploring (Ciarkowski, 2022). First, you must name the emotion others are feeling. Let's use the same example we saw in the previous section. So, let's imagine your best friend texts you that they have a family trip next weekend and adds a sad face. To confirm you correctly understood their emotion, you can text them something like, "Are you frustrated because you can't go out?" You must be as precise as possible and avoid using words like happiness, sadness, or anger, which are very generic and feel like less manageable and solvable emotions. After naming, you must understand their point of view. Therefore, you must avoid sentences like, "I understand the situation," because you probably don't if you're not aware of the specific details and circumstances. Just encourage them to tell you more about what happened and how they feel. The next step consists of showing respect by appreciating their efforts. For example, you can tell your best friend something like, "I can see you really care about your family." This way, you'll help them look at the bright side and feel better (Ciarkowski, 2022).

Then, you must keep supporting them by finding a solution together. In the example of your best friend, you can tell them they should enjoy the weekend and promise them you'll go out together the next one and do something fun. You can highlight the fact that you'll spend a lot of time together and catch up on the latest events in your lives. You can also suggest you do an activity they love. The last step of responding to emotional cues consists of further exploring the situation. In other words, you can ask them more questions to analyze how they feel more in-depth or lighten the conversation with jokes and topics that might make your best friend feel better. In the end, you'll notice they feel much calmer and are positive toward their future. They'll also know you care about them and you look forward to going out with them next time (Ciarkowski, 2022).

CASE STUDIES: EMPATHY

How does empathy work in action? Let's look at some examples. Imagine your partner is overwhelmed by an exam they have to take next week. They feel like they can study all day for weeks and still not pass it. They feel hopeless and don't want to do anything next weekend except stay in their bedroom all day and keep studying. You see they're in a bad mood and look disheartened. You've never faced a similar situation because exams usually don't make you feel as stressed as it happens to them. However, you try to put yourself in their shoes and think about what you could do to cheer them up. You know they enjoy Indian food, and sometimes, they ask you to help them study. Therefore, you tell them next Saturday night you'll stay at home with them: You'll order Indian food for dinner and study together. Your partner looks surprised and excited about your offer. They accept it and immediately feel much better.

Another situation in which you can show empathy is with your classmates. Let's imagine you're excellent at Science, and one of your classmates asks for your help. Initially, you're reluctant because you don't have a lot of free time and want to spend your weekends with your friends—not studying Science with your classmates. Moreover, you don't talk to them a lot and don't get along well, so you would avoid spending time together. However, your class-mate looks desperate and needs to understand Science to pass the exam. They really need your help and think you're the only one that can give them a hand. If you show empathy, you end up saying you'll help them and organize to meet their needs and yours. If you don't show empathy, you keep telling them you can't study with them and put your interests over theirs.

DIY

Do you feel like practicing becoming more empathetic? Try the following activity. Choose a positive and a negative scenario and write empathetic responses for each. Put yourself in the shoes of the people involved and imagine how they might be feeling. For example, you can listen to your parents' conversations about work and choose situations that can help you practice empathy. Think about how your parents and other people involved might feel. You can do the same with all sorts of scenarios, such as TV news, people chatting on the street, your friends telling you about their lives, and so on. Thanks to this exercise, you'll learn how to express empathy in various situations and how it's essential in all aspects of our lives.

In this chapter, we focused on empathy. We learned what it is and how we can see it in others. In general, being empathetic means being able to put ourselves in others' shoes without judging them. We also discovered that empathy allows us to create deeper connections with the people around us because it makes them feel profoundly understood and appreciated for who they are. Next, we learned techniques to show empathy over text. We discovered how to express empathy and recognize essential emotional cues. Finally, we looked at real-life examples where we can show empathy and a straightforward activity that can help us become more empathetic. In Chapter 5, we'll discuss the topic of conflicts and how to properly handle them online.

A LITTLE HELP FOR YOUR FRIENDS

"The greatest gift that you can give yourself is a little bit of your own attention."

— ANTHONY J. D'ANGELO

I hope that by this stage in the book, you're realizing that when you have a better understanding of social media and its nuances, digital communication can become your superpower. You're no longer a slave to it, anxiously waiting for likes or worrying about what that one emoji meant for hours on end. Instead, you're in control, and you can use it as a tool with which to communicate effectively and bolster your relationships.

As you do this, it's quite likely that you'll become more aware of the gaps in your friends' knowledge when it comes to social media. You might even find yourself getting annoyed with their online etiquette or the amount of time they spend on their phone when you're hanging out.

Try to be patient if this happens, and remember where you were when you started this journey. You can even tell them a bit about what you've learned and how it's improved your life, and better yet, you can give them a copy of the book so they can make these discoveries for themselves.

Our phones will rule us if we're not careful, yet they're powerful tools when we use them well. My goal is to make sure as many young people as I can are in charge of their devices and not the other way around. And I'd like to take this opportunity to ask for your help in reaching more of them. The best part is that it's easy. All it takes is a short review.

By leaving a review of this book on Amazon, you'll show other young people how to navigate the digital landscape, improving their communication and relationships in the process.

Your words will act as a signpost, showing new readers where they can find the information they're looking for.

Thank you so much for your support. Now, let's get back to the task in hand!

Scan the QR code below

5

NAVIGATING CONFLICT DIGITALLY

66 *How well we communicate is not determined by how well we say things but how well we are understood.*

— ANDREW GROVE

The fifth strategy consists of properly handling conflicts online. Sometimes, they might come out of nowhere with our loved ones just because we misunderstood one of their messages or vice versa, as we already learned in Chapter 2. Other times, one of our followers just leaves a negative comment that makes us feel personally attacked and react inappropriately, thus uselessly lengthening an argument. That's why it's essential to understand how conflicts work online and how to respectfully solve them, as we'll learn in the following sections. We'll also reflect on how to give and receive constructive feedback online and look at a practical activity that helps us manage conflicts by providing useful feedback.

COMMON SOURCES OF CONFLICT

Where and Why It Happens

A conflict between you and others might arise online for various reasons. For example, you might use social media differently and have different personalities. Let's imagine your best friend is used to looking at their phone every five minutes and immediately replying to all the messages they receive while you only look at it when you have some free time. Therefore, you have different expectations concerning response time. They might expect you to answer in a few minutes and get anxious if you don't, while you might send them a message and not look at your phone for hours. Such situations might cause conflicts because both you and your best friend might get upset about how you handle social media and messages. The same can happen with your parents, who might have different expectations on how to use the phone. A common problem among social media users is information overload, which indicates the urge to keep up with all the latest updates. If we don't manage to do it, we feel overwhelmed or left behind. If you don't look at your phone on the weekend because you are busy, you might find a lot of notifications when you wake up on Monday. Conflicts might arise because you feel frustrated while your friends talk about things you don't know.

You might also find yourself in an argument because of environmental factors. As already discussed, we all struggle to recognize emotional cues, and we can't rely on fundamental non-verbal cues that can help us understand the tone and context of a specific situation. It's easy to misunderstand a message or a silence online. When you text someone, can you easily understand if they're serious or sarcastic? When they don't reply to your messages, are they just busy doing something else, or are they angry at you? Another common source of conflict is anonymity. When you talk to strangers online, you know you'll probably never meet them, and so do they. Therefore, you both feel free to use whatever language you want—even insults. You feel less responsible for the words you use and think you don't hurt anyone. It's much easier to complain about your teachers online than in front of them, isn't it? But what if you publish a post on your profile, and they see it? You might face the real consequences of your actions online. You might also create a useless conflict among the students at your school who look at your post.

Conflict Doesn't Have to Be Negative

How do you perceive conflicts? Do you try to avoid them or think that they're bad? Your attitude plays an essential role in properly dealing with conflicts. If you keep avoiding them, you'll have to face them sooner or later and won't possess the skills you need to solve them. If you think they're negative because they ruin relationships, you might deal with them with the wrong attitude and make them become endless arguments with no apparent purpose. If you want to successfully handle conflicts, you must change your mindset and perceive them as opportunities and something positive that can enhance your relationships.

Positive or healthy conflict differs from negative one in many aspects. The former is characterized by tolerance and collaboration, which means that both parties involved in the conflict try their best to understand the other's point of view and find a compromise that can benefit both. They carefully listen to each other, express their opinions, and elaborate a solution together. Negative

BEYOND EMOJIS | 91

conflicts are usually characterized by a lack of problem-solving skills that puts both parties in an unfavorable position. In most cases, neither of them manages to achieve what they want, and they end up feeling worse than before.

The main difference between a healthy and a negative conflict is the outcome. In the first case, both parties win because they benefit from the solution while in the second, one wins and the other loses. The reasons why you must learn how to solve conflicts are varied. For example, you build stronger relationships by boosting trust and cooperation between you and the people involved in the conflict. You also save a lot of time and energy as you manage to successfully deal with arguments without unnecessarily lengthening them. Finally, positive conflict management improves your emotional intelligence as you learn to listen and understand others.

As you can see, healthy conflicts have a positive impact on your overall well-being. That's why you must change your attitude and start considering conflicts positively. You can take advantage of them to improve your life.

RESOLVING CONFLICTS RESPECTFULLY IN DIGITAL SPACES

What to Do

What can you do practically to enhance your conflict management skills online? The first thing you must remember is that you have an advantage compared to face-to-face conflicts: You can think. When we argue in person, especially if the topic is sensitive, we tend to talk without thinking. We just say everything that crosses our minds without considering the other person's feelings and reactions. Pausing and reflecting in a face-to-face conflict is almost impossible as we need to be patient, calm, and understanding at the same time. Conversely, you have all the time you need online. You don't have to answer immediately, but you can take a break and think about your next actions. What could you reply to end the argument peacefully? If you say what you have in mind, will you clarify the situation and solve the issue? These are just examples of questions you can ask yourself when you notice a conflict has arisen online. But there's much more you can do. Here, you will find a step-by-step guide to properly face arguments online.

1. Listen:

As always, the best and most effective advice is to listen. Remember not to put your needs first and give the other person time to express themselves and say what they want. This way, they'll notice your proactive attitude and be more likely to listen to you, too. Show interest in their opinion and ask clarifying questions, as you learned in the previous chapters.

2. Use "I" statements:

Whenever we find ourselves in conflicts, we tend to attack the other person and don't focus on the most important issue. If you argue with your parents, you might tell them something like, "You never understand me. You never consider my opinion," and so on. In response, your parents might get even angrier and ground you. That's because you've used "You" statements and described how you perceive them, not who they are in reality. To solve conflicts peacefully, you must clearly express your point of view. For instance, you can say something like, "I feel misunderstood when you say such words," or "I feel frustrated when you don't consider my opinion." Can you notice the difference just by reading the sentences? I guess so.

3. Get to the heart of the matter:

Most conflicts arise because there's an inner problem you're not aware of or you don't want to see. Once you overcome that barrier, you can respectfully deal with all sorts of arguments. Whenever someone starts a fight, and you don't understand the reason, investigate further. When you feel nervous or angry and want to avoid a conflict, try asking yourself why you feel like that and go to the roots of the problem.

4. Agree and compromise:

No matter how your opinions differ—you can always find common ground. Consider the other person's point of view and explicitly agree with them when you think they're right. I know it might sound difficult, but it will help you solve the conflict. Even if it's something insignificant, tell them you understand and think they're right, then express your opinion. Finally, try to find a compromise that can benefit both parties.

When you start a conflict online, you might do it publicly if you or others reply to your posts where everyone can see what you write. To make sure you effectively solve the argument, gently ask the other party if you can discuss the issue privately. This way, you'll have more chance to avoid useless escalations and other people interfering with your attempt to manage the conflict.

When to Walk Away

When you notice a negative conflict, you must do your best to make it positive. Follow all the above suggestions and change your attitude to properly face arguments. However, in some cases, all your attempts might be fruitless. Some people try to solve conflicts, while others just cause them and don't care about effectively dealing with them. They're so competitive they just want to win and be right. In such cases, there's nothing you can do. That's why you must learn when and how to drop it and just walk away from the conflict. It might look counterproductive, but sometimes, it's the only solution.

To understand when to walk away, you must first clarify the difference between an argument and a discussion. A discussion occurs when both parties feel free to express their opinions, and the exchange is open-ended. In other words, there's no competition or someone who wants to win over the other. An example of a discussion is when you ask your partner what they want to do during the weekend, and you reflect on it together. You examine various options and choose the one that you both like. When you find yourself in an argument, you don't feel free to say what you want; you carefully choose your next words. You feel threatened and feel like you should defend yourself from a personal attack. Your body naturally activates the fight-or-flight response, and you prepare to respond to the attack or run away. Even when you're online, you can understand when a discussion is becoming an argument, or a conflict is about to arise.

It is easy to notice a change in others' messages. Maybe they've texted you for minutes or hours and suspiciously grow quiet at a certain point in the conversation. Otherwise, they start using more aggressive language, such as adding periods at the end of each sentence or using "okay" too often to answer your messages. Let's take the previous example of you discussing what to do on the weekend with your partner on WhatsApp. It looks like they agree with you going out with your friends as you haven't seen them in a while, so you change the subject. You ask them questions, but they only reply something like, "Okay, it's the same," or "You choose," and keep adding a period at the end of each sentence. You can sense there's something wrong.

So, what can you do next? If transforming the negative conflict into positive is not enough, just walk away. It's not hard online, as you can just mute notifications and not look at your phone for a while. When you take it back after some time, you might have probably forgotten about the previous argument. Alternatively, you can be honest with the other person and end the conversation using words such as, "I feel like this conversation is going nowhere as we're just repeating our opinions without finding a compromise, so I prefer not participating anymore. Thank you." The previous sentence is particularly helpful in case of online disputes with strangers. When you argue with your loved ones through text, you might use a different approach. You can be honest with them and tell them you prefer discussing the issue face-to-face, as it's always better and can increase the probability of finding a compromise. This way, you end the argument without being too rude, have time to think about the issue, and choose the right words when you see them in person.

GIVING AND RECEIVING CONSTRUCTIVE FEEDBACK ONLINE

Giving

Dealing with feedback is no easy task, as you probably found out on your own. Have you ever tried to give constructive feedback to someone and ended up in a fight because they misunderstood your words? If so, you shouldn't worry, as it's a pretty common situation. Giving constructive feedback is a fine art that's hard to master— but not impossible. The secret is to find the perfect balance between clarity and harshness. If you provide generic feedback or try to be too polite, others might misinterpret your words and think you're just giving a piece of advice they can ignore. If you're too direct, you might look harsh and make others feel defensive, thus risking provoking an argument. So, how can you become excellent at giving feedback without hurting others? You must follow some straightforward steps.

1. Check if the receiver is ready:

The first thing you must do to give constructive feedback is make sure the person is ready to receive it. If you're in the middle of an argument and they look agitated, then it's not the best time to provide feedback. If the conflict has already ended and they look calm, you can give it a try. When you think they're ready, don't just throw your opinion at them, but gently ask them if they feel like discussing their behavior and thoughts. This way, they know what's about to occur, so you don't catch them off guard, and they feel like they can participate in the conversation and not just passively receive your feedback.

2. Be specific:

Before giving feedback, reflect on what you want to say and make sure you include all elements of the story (who, what, when, and where). The best way to give constructive feedback is to be clear, concise, and direct. If you're vague, the receiver might not understand what you want from them and may not implement your suggestions.

Therefore, giving feedback would be completely useless. Let's imagine your sibling made you feel irritated because they mocked you in front of your friends. To give them constructive feedback, you must start by telling them something like, "Are you willing to discuss a situation that made me feel irritated? Do you remember what happened yesterday? We were outside of school with my friends, and you said that thing in front of all of them." This way, your sibling will easily understand the situation you refer to.

3. Share your perception:

After clarifying what you're talking about, you must provide your take on what happened. How did your sibling make you feel? In this case, too, you must be precise and concise so that they clearly understand what went wrong. Don't use accusatory language that might make them feel defensive and prefer "I" statements over "You" sentences so that they don't feel attacked. Here's an example of what you can tell your sibling: "Yesterday, you made me feel irritated because it looked like you were mocking me in front of my friends. I didn't like your behavior and wanted you to stop it. Can you please tell me why you behaved like that?" In addition to sharing your point of view on what happened, you can show them you want to understand their perspective by asking them why they behaved in a certain way and listening to their words.

4. Be realistic:

Whenever you're ready to give feedback, make sure you're realistic and give actionable recommendations. Just telling your sibling to never repeat the same behavior again might not be enough. You must tell them how you would like them to behave in front of your friends. After letting them talk and explain why they did what they did, think about a way to solve the issue that can benefit both of you. You can use the step-by-step guide in the section about what you can do to solve conflicts respectfully. Make sure your feedback is tangible, concrete, clear, easy, and fast to put into practice. Avoid using words like "always" or "never", and let the receiver know you would like to see a change in their behavior in the next days, weeks, or months. Offer various alternatives and don't ask them impossible things.

5. Avoid lectures:

While giving feedback, remember you're talking to another human being. As you wouldn't want others to give you lectures on how you should live your life and behave, so the people you love. Giving feedback is a two-way process in which you must listen to the other person and try to understand their point of view. To make sure you give constructive feedback, you must listen to what they're willing to do to improve and how they perceive the event that made you feel bad.

Receiving

Giving constructive feedback to allow the other person to accept and implement it is hard, just like receiving good advice. Whenever someone says something about our thoughts or behaviors, we get defensive and feel like they're criticizing our personalities and way of being. To properly receive feedback, you must let go of the idea that people want to criticize you and think of it as a way of becoming a better person. The more feedback you learn to accept, the more you'll improve and feel happier about yourself. To make sure you properly receive feedback, you must follow the next steps.

1. Listen:

We unintentionally become defensive when someone openly discusses our behaviors and opinions, but it won't help us look at the feedback in the right way. When someone's about to provide useful advice, we must take a deep breath, relax, and get ready to accept whatever they say. Remember, nobody likes being criticized, so no matter what feedback you receive—you won't feel excited after you've heard it. Once you accept it, you have the right attitude to listen to the person giving feedback. Let them talk and express their opinions as you would like them to do with you. Try to understand the situation and ask them to clarify questions if you're not sure you correctly understand everything they're saying. Go as deep as you can to have a clear picture of what happened. You can also ask for examples or stories that can help you understand what you can do to improve.

2. Process feedback:

Don't rush to implement the feedback you receive, but take all the time you need, even days or weeks, to reflect on what happened. Analyze your behavior, the reasons and roots behind it, how it made others feel, what you can do to improve, and what other people suggest. While reflecting, think about the feedback-giver's perspective. Consider their motives, intent, and position. For example, feedback from your teachers always has the intent to help you get better grades and improve your well-being. But what about others? We tend to perceive feedback as a mirror of our behavior, but it actually depends on others' needs, values, and impressions. For these reasons, feedback isn't always constructive and helpful. Sometimes, it's just a reflection of how others would like you to be to make their lives easier. That's why you must ask yourself if you trust the person who gives you feedback and if they're genuinely interested in helping you improve.

The last step of properly receiving feedback consists of implementing the advice people give you. We'll look at it in the next section.

Implementing

How can you successfully implement feedback others give you? Here are the steps you must follow.

1. Ask people around:

To process the feedback you receive and make sure the person who gives it to you has good intentions, you can ask others what they think about it. Choose people you trust and love, like your family or friends, and ask about their opinions. Maybe one of your classmates told you to stop answering all the questions the teachers asked the class because you looked like a nerd. If you don't discuss the situation with somebody else, you might think they're right, and you should change your behavior. Conversely, talking about it with your family and friends might help you see the circumstances from another perspective and accept your behavior. If you notice that all (or almost all) your loved ones agree with the feedback you received, then it's probably helpful. If you notice some disagreements, then the feedback you receive is not as constructive as you might believe.

2. Look at patterns:

If your loved ones agree you should change your behavior, do you notice a specific pattern, like something you say or do, that irritates them more than anything else? If you ask your loved ones how they perceive you when you talk about your grades, you might find out they all think you act as if you're the cleverest person in the world and brag about them. Therefore, you might notice a pattern you can change.

3. Develop a strategy and set goals:

Gather all the feedback you receive and plan your action. Consider others' suggestions, what looks more feasible, and what you're willing to do. To develop a successful strategy, you must set achievable goals and identify all the steps you must make to reach them. This way, you'll also have the necessary motivation to face all the challenges you'll find in your growth path. Let's imagine your friends told you to send them fewer memes throughout the day, as you tend to text them a lot to talk about superficial things, like cute puppies doing hilarious stuff. You bombard them with messages, and they receive many notifications. Once you understand and accept their feedback, you can work on it. For example, you can consider the daily hours you dedicate to social media and look at all the messages you send to your friends. Then, develop a strategy to improve your behavior. First, think about the big picture and what you want to achieve in one year. Then, focus on the smaller steps, which are your monthly, weekly, and daily achievements. Obviously, you can't stop using social media from one day to another, and that's not the goal you want to achieve. Maybe you can stop following some pages that only share superficial posts, or you can look at social media less often. Think about the best course of action for you and put it into practice.

After developing a strategy, you can ask for support and share your plan with your loved ones. This way, you'll feel more accountable for your actions and motivated to do your best. Moreover, receiving help from others can only make you achieve your goals more rapidly.

DIY

Are you curious to put into practice what you've learned in this chapter? You can reflect on and understand the difference between an online and a face-to-face conflict, thanks to the next activity. Think of a recent disagreement or miscommunication you had online. Write down your perspective and then write how you would provide constructive feedback if you were addressing the issue in person. You can try this exercise on your own or involve one of your friends. For instance, you can recall a recent argument you had online and think about how it could have developed in person. Did you use the same words and behave in the same way? Do you notice a difference in your reactions and replies? Think about the above questions to enhance your understanding of conflicts.

In this chapter, we discovered everything we need to successfully deal with conflicts online. Arguments can arise because of personal differences in handling social media or environmental factors, such as the absence of non-verbal cues. To properly handle conflicts, we might change our attitude and consider them as something positive. A healthy conflict involves considering all points of view and respecting each other. How can we solve arguments respectfully? We must listen, use "I" statements, get to the roots of the problem, and find a compromise together. When that's not enough, we should just walk away to avoid endless and useless conflicts. Next, we found out the best ways to give, receive, and implement feedback online and learned a useful exercise to understand the difference between online and face-to-face arguments. In the next chapter, we'll discover how to strengthen relationships and increase meaningful interactions online.

6

BEYOND THE SCREEN - STRENGTHENING RELATIONSHIPS

When people talk, listen completely. Most people never listen.

— ERNEST HEMINGWAY

Throughout the book, we inevitably discussed relationships and how we can improve them, thanks to the techniques discussed. Now, we'll take a closer look at them and discover everything we need to know about how to build and maintain long-lasting relationships online and offline. First, we'll examine why they matter and how we can go beyond superficial interactions to build meaningful relationships. Second, we'll learn how to make stronger connections by strengthening both online and offline interactions. Next, we'll find out how to boost online friendships, and we'll look at personal stories of online friendships that flourished thanks to excellent communication. Finally, we'll find a practical activity that helps us retain what we learned in the chapter.

THE IMPORTANCE OF RELATIONSHIPS

Why Relationships Matter

Has someone ever told you something like, "Go out there and make new friends. It's easier than you think?" If you struggle to build new friendships, you might believe you're a mess and must find a way to become more extroverted and confident in interacting with others. However, there's one thing we all tend to forget: Not all relationships are the same. You can have plenty of friends and always know you'll do something on weekends and still feel lonely and stressed. That's because quality is more important than quantity. You might have already heard it and thought it was useless advice, but it's not. Relationships have the power to improve our lives or make us feel worse. If you're in an unhealthy relationship, you might feel stressed and anxious and face conflicts more often than you should. Let's imagine you just made a new friend: They're extroverted, enjoy going to parties, and make you meet a lot of new people. You might believe they're the best friend you'll ever have. At the same time, they never ask you what you want to do but just tell you to accompany them to parties. They interact with other people and never let you talk or leave you alone while they have fun. As much as you might love them, they make you feel lonely and not appreciated. You feel like you can't be yourself and just have to do what they want. Whenever you bring up the issue with them, they don't listen to you as if your opinion doesn't count at all. In the long term, your mental and physical health can suffer from such a situation.

That's why you must choose your friends wisely and prefer having fewer but stronger relationships. Healthy relationships help you live a longer and more satisfying life. They reduce your stress levels because they make you feel protected, appreciated for who you are, and accepted. If you're in a healthy relationship, you increase your levels of self-confidence because the other person lets you discover yourself, what you like, and what you don't like. Even if they have their own opinion, which might differ from yours, they validate and respect your ideas. Healthy relationships also encourage you to try new things and become a better person. If your best friend eats healthier than you do, you might end up paying more attention to the food you eat, thanks to them. Being in a healthy relationship can also give you a sense of belonging and purpose because you know someone cares for you, and you want to show them you care, too. Moreover, healthy relationships support you, even in the hardest times. Good friends always offer a shoulder to cry on and listen to your needs and wants. You know they'll do everything for you just like you would for them.

Going Beyond Superficial Interactions

Since digital communication has spread around the world, the way we build relationships has changed. Nowadays, it's easier to make new friends online, but it's more difficult to build meaningful relationships. You might chat every day with a lot of different people and still talk about memes and nothing else. Having deep and meaningful conversations online is much harder than in person. For this reason, you might end up lacking the depth we all need in our lives. As funny as it might be to share funny memes and pictures with your online friends and followers, it's not enough to make you live a fulfilling life. You also need something more, and that's why you must learn how to build meaningful relationships.

First, you must let go of the idea that you're "weird." In an era where everyone shares perfect pictures of their amazing life, we all feel different and crave to be normal. We think we must take the same wonderful pictures to be happy. If we don't, it means our lives are miserable. Have you ever thought about what's behind those photos and deep descriptions you see on social media? Are those people really happy, or do they suffer like you? Nobody's perfect, and, in a certain way, we're all weird. Normality simply doesn't exist. You might envy a person because they have more followers than you and always have a lot of likes and comments on their profile. In reality, they might suffer and think that the best way not to think about their troubles is to post on their social media and look perfect.

If you want to build meaningful connections, you must realize you're no different from your peers. You must accept yourself for who you are or, in other words, be authentic. You mustn't be afraid of looking vulnerable or imperfect on your social media because we all are. Moreover, being authentic helps you connect with people who have the same viewpoint and like the same things. If you show others your true self, you'll be more likely to be rejected by those who differ from you and find like-minded people. Obviously, you can't be liked by everyone, so you must choose the people you want in your life to feel more satisfied and happier. Those who will see your authentic self will also be more likely to open up with you and share important details of their lives. Consequently, you'll build deeper and more meaningful connections. We'll get back to the topic of authenticity and vulnerability in the last chapter.

INTEGRATING ONLINE AND OFFLINE COMMUNICATION

How Does This Work

Both online and offline communication have pros and cons. If you prefer offline communication, you might wait for days to talk to your best friend because you must meet them in person. At the same time, you're 100% sure they'll dedicate time to yourself and listen to what you want to tell them. You also know you can rely on non-verbal cues that help you understand their opinion on your words. If you choose online communication, you can send a message in a few seconds and receive a reply in a few minutes or hours—depending on the frequency with which your loved ones look at their smartphones. However, you're aware they won't dedicate the same amount of time they'll dedicate if you meet in person. In fact, they might answer your message while looking at other chats, posts, comments, and likes. Moreover, you can't completely trust their words because you can't see their immediate reactions to what you tell them. They might appear excited in the message and still not care about your words. For all the above reasons, just online or offline communication isn't enough to build a strong connection: You need both.

How can you integrate online and offline communication? The essential element is to be there for your loved ones and do regular check-ins. You mustn't feel forced to immediately answer the messages you receive, but you must show you care about your loved ones. If you wait some time to reply, apologize and explain what happened so they'll know you were busy. Instead of asking simple questions like, "How are you?" go deeper and ask them how their day was, if they did something interesting or funny, if they learned something new, and so on. For example, you can ask your best friend how the classes went, if the teachers explained fascinating topics, or if they practiced some exercises. To build meaningful connections, you must alternate between online and offline communication. You can text your best friend during the week because you're both busy studying and doing extracurricular activities, and you can go out with them on weekends. This way, you'll have the opportunity to discuss superficial topics online and face more sensitive ones in person. You can follow the same approach in all sorts of relationships. Just remember to regularly check on them and ask follow-up questions. Finally, listening is just as important as talking. Therefore, you can tell something about yourself to encourage others to do the same. One of your friends might be embarrassed because they didn't pass an exam for the first time. To comfort them and build a stronger connection, you might tell them about the time you got a low grade and how you faced the situation.

BOOSTING ONLINE FRIENDSHIPS

Making meaningful friendships online seems hard, as conversations usually don't last long, and they consist of exchanging memes and laughing together. However, online friendships aren't impossible. Don't take for granted the fact that you'll never make good friends online. Conversely, see digital communication as an opportunity to boost your friendships. How can you do it? First, you must look for friend-making platforms, which are similar to dating apps but specifically designed to help people meet and make new friends. Just search on the internet, and you'll find tons of apps with different purposes, like playing sports or getting to know your neighbors. You can also use dating apps like Tinder to meet new people, but I suggest you try friend-making platforms where you're more likely to meet people who want to achieve your same goal.

In addition, or alternatively to friend-making platforms, you can try online communities and forums. No matter what's your hobby or interest—you'll find an online forum about it. There, you can talk about your passions with people who like the same things you enjoy and have fun discussing them. You can start by participating in group discussions or commenting on some posts. You don't have to immediately direct message someone, which might be awkward or too scary for you. It's also a good way of getting to know the other participants and finding out who you get along better with. After commenting on some posts and sharing your opinion, you can write to the person you find more interesting and tell them you'd like to know them better because it looks like you have a lot of things in common. If they're willing to become your friend, then you're lucky. If they're not, you just need to find another person who is. Keep in mind you can't be liked by everyone, and not every person is interested in making new friends, so don't give up.

Once you've made a new friend online, you can keep nurturing the relationship and take it to the next level. As human beings, we need something more than just exchanging memes and texting. At some point, it's likely you or your new friend would ask to meet in person, especially if you don't live too far away from each other. Meeting face-to-face will allow you to blend online and offline communication and deepen the relationship. First, make sure you want to take this leap. Consider what you have in common with your online friend and the way you engage in back-and-forth exchanges. Do you discuss various topics at length? Do you have fun together? Do you manage to talk about both superficial and sensitive issues? If the answer to the above questions is always "Yes," you should try to take the friendship to the next level. Just keep in mind not to rush things and make sure you both feel comfortable with each other. For this reason, I suggest you regularly text your friend to get to know them better and get a feel for their daily life, how they react to various situations, and what their routine is. Obviously, you must do the same. Moreover, you must take one step at a time. If you're used to texting them on social media like Instagram or TikTok, you might want to exchange numbers before meeting in person. This way, the relationship becomes more intimate but not as much as a face-to-face meeting would be. You can also make video calls to see how they look and discover more about their body language and non-verbal communication.

When you think you're ready to meet your online friend, ask them if they feel the same and decide when and where to talk face-to-face. I suggest you choose a public space where you both feel safe and comfortable. When you meet them in person, remember to manage your expectations. You might have created your own image of how your friend might look and behave in real life, or you might expect to immediately talk about all the interesting topics you usually discuss online. Well, face-to-face meetings rarely go as planned. You might feel a bit embarrassed in the beginning, or they might look different from what you expected. Allow yourself some time to calm down after the initial excitement of finally meeting your online friend. Don't get discouraged by the fact that your friend and you might look like two strangers who never talked before. Just relax, make yourself and your friend comfortable, and enjoy the time together. After a few minutes, you'll both feel at ease and start talking as you're used to doing online. If you feel like you clicked and had fun with your online friend, stay in touch with them. To build long-lasting friendships, you must make sure you always check on them, keep talking, and meet again in the future. This way, your online friendship will easily become a deep and strong connection.

CASE STUDIES: PERSONAL STORIES OF ONLINE FRIENDSHIPS

Do you struggle to imagine an online friendship that becomes a meaningful and long-lasting relationship? You might not know it, but there are hundreds of stories of online friends who become besties thanks to excellent communication. Research has found that in 2015, 57% of teens made new friends online, and one in three decided to meet face-to-face (Hirschlag, 2017). Do you want to know some real-life stories? Here are a few.

You might have heard about the story that went viral on Reddit and involved two little girls. Their mothers are friends but live far away from each other, so they don't manage to meet. Moreover, they both have very busy lives and must take care of their daughters. This doesn't stop them from texting and video calling every once in a while.

Their daughters meet, too, and become friends. After years of seeing each other online, one mother finally has the time to meet her friend and decides to surprise her. Finally, their daughters can meet face-to-face. Instead of awkward silences or embarrassment, they immediately hug for a long time. Over the years, they keep video calling and meeting in person. They become true friends both in the digital and real world.

But this is just an example. Some adults met online because they ran the same business and wanted to make new connections with colleagues. Then, they discovered they had other things in common in addition to their job and became best friends. Others found their love or best friends on online gaming platforms or fans' forums. Most of them started chatting when they were just teenagers and are still friends now. Another fascinating story talks about a girl who was deliberately excluded from a birthday party by her friends. A guy posted a video online to warn her, and it went viral. When the video finally reached her, she was upset because of her friends' behaviors. But people online never left her alone and kept inviting her to birthday parties, weddings, and all sorts of events. That's what made that girl have an innovative idea. She decided to organize meetings in person for everyone who felt lonely in Central Park, New York. She posted TikTok videos to inform her followers and managed to gather hundreds of people. Now, she organizes meetups all over the U.S.A. thanks to the "No More Lonely Friends" gatherings.

Digital communication has the potential to improve your life by helping you make new friends—you just need to look in the right place and keep an open mind. You can't never know who'll become your best friend online.

DIY

You can reflect on the meaningful connections you've built over the years by practicing the next activity. Scroll through your old messages with a close friend or family member. Pick out a few meaningful conversations that made you feel connected. Reflect on the evolution of your digital relationship and consider ways to recreate those moments of depth and connection. Think about how the relationship has changed since then and if online and offline communication affected it in some way.

In this chapter, we discussed ways to improve our relationships in the digital era. We learned that we don't need to have hundreds of friends to feel satisfied, but we must give importance to quality rather than quantity. We also discovered that online communication is not only bad but can help us create meaningful connections if we use it wisely and integrate it with offline meetings. We found ways in which we can boost our online friendships and examples of online friends who managed to build strong connections. Finally, we learned a practical activity. We can try to discover how our relationships have changed over the years and how offline and online communication has affected them. In the next chapter, we'll discuss a rather unusual topic: Digital etiquette.

7

DIGITAL ETIQUETTE AND RESPECT

We are stronger when we listen and smarter when we share.

— RANIA AL-ABDULLAH

H ave you ever heard of digital etiquette? You might think of it as something boring and compare it to the classical social etiquette that forces you to think, behave, and appear in certain ways. Digital etiquette is much more than that, as it shows you how to respectfully interact with others online. The seventh strategy you'll learn in this chapter will help you master the most important digital etiquette skills you need to succeed. Thanks to them, you'll be able to communicate online healthily and productively. In the next sections, you'll discover what digital etiquette is and why it matters. You'll learn how to address common forms of negativity online, such as cyberbullying and trolling, and how to maintain a positive online presence. At the end of the chapter, you'll also find a practical activity to put into practice what you learn.

DIGITAL ETIQUETTE 101

What Is It?

Digital etiquette is also defined as netiquette and is a set of rules we should all follow to make sure the internet is a safe place for us all. Like social etiquette, it's characterized by ways in which we should all behave, such as making good choices or respecting others. In general, the basic rules that apply in real life also apply online. In fact, we should treat others as we would like to be treated, we should be kind and include everyone, and we should discuss private and sensitive issues outside of group chats or public posts where everyone can read (*What Is Digital Etiquette?*, 2019). But what are the specific rules of digital etiquette? There are many, and they're all useful.

For example, we should avoid using language that might be perceived as strong or offensive. If we don't agree with someone, we mustn't tell them they're stupid or something worse, but we must accept their opinions and express ours respectfully. Moreover, we shouldn't post or send material that might be considered inappropriate. We should also remember to read before writing, as we listen before we speak. Before expressing our opinions, we must make sure we correctly understand what others write so that we can reply appropriately. Moreover, we should stay on topic and avoid mixing up different issues. In fact, others might feel confused by our words and attacked. For this reason, it's essential that we pay attention to what we write and don't include more topics in the same conversation. Before sending the final message, we should also read it again and again to check for grammar errors and make sure we correctly express what we think and feel. We must ask ourselves if our message could be misinterpreted and what we can do to make it clearer. Moreover, we must never plagiarize and always give credit to the original authors. The temptation to steal someone else's tweet, quote, or meme is huge, but we must resist it. Whenever we see a beautiful picture or post online, we must make sure we mention its author (Collins, n.d.).

After all, we wouldn't want others to steal our ideas and memes, would we?

The above rules give you an idea of what digital etiquette entails. If you think about it, it's not too different from the social etiquette we use in real life. Sometimes, we forget the real and digital worlds are the same. We tend to believe we're allowed to do whatever we want online, so we behave differently from what we would do in our real lives. Once we realize the real and digital worlds correspond, we can behave appropriately in both.

Why Does It Matter?

Why would you want to follow and respect the rules of digital etiquette? As boring as it might look, it's extremely helpful and improves your life. What do you usually do when your phone rings while you're having a face-to-face conversation? Do you answer it or keep talking? Research suggests that 39% of teens would answer (*Digital Etiquette*, 2016). You can find many stories online about teens and adults who used their phones inappropriately and didn't follow digital etiquette. In some cases, they answered their phone during job interviews and asked the interviewer to leave the room because the conversation was private. Would you do the same or understand that's not an appropriate behavior? If you wouldn't do it, then you know how to respect digital etiquette. It also means you're aware of how inappropriate behavior online can affect people around you. Imagine how the interviewers might have felt in those moments and how they might have behaved. I guess they didn't hire those people.

The way you behave in your digital life has a real impact. If you don't pay attention to your behavior online, you might contribute to making the digital world a place of misinformed facts, cyberbullying, and scamming. Remember, all your followers can see what you post and might be influenced by it. Therefore, make sure your posts align with your values and don't spread false facts. If you want to share an interesting article, but the topic is controversial, and you're not sure all your followers will correctly interpret it, then you shouldn't share it. If you want, you can share it with your closest friends and loved ones who know you well and understand your point of view. Others might misunderstand your words and believe you're a bad person even if you aren't. Moreover, you mustn't cyberbully others as it can have real consequences. The person who's bullied might get hurt by your behavior and decide to take dangerous actions in their real life. We all have the right to use technology, but we also have responsibilities. If we want to be good digital citizens, we must treat the digital world as we treat the real one. The way we use social media can influence others. If we want to live in a kinder and more respectful digital world, we must be kind and respectful of ourselves. We must make sure everyone who uses the internet feels secure and accepted for who they are.

COMMON ARES OF ONLINE NEGATIVITY

Addressing Cyberbullying

In 2017, 17% of young people reported being bullied online (Lockett, 2022). We can assume this percentage will keep increasing as social media become more and more popular and we all use it in our daily lives. Cyberbullying is a form of bullying that occurs online, especially on messaging apps, social media platforms, online forums, or video-gaming communities. Sometimes, cyberbullying can become so aggressive that it results in criminal activity, such as in cases of stalking or discriminatory harassment. In fact, there are many types of cyberbullying. Harassment is the most typical one, as it includes elements like threatening or offensive messages. Flaming is the act of sending angry and inflammatory messages to one person to make them react negatively and continue the argument. People who practice flaming just want to provoke others to make them engage back in unhealthy fights. Cyberstalking is the online version of stalking. If, in real life, a stalker would keep following a specific person online, they monitor all their online activities. Therefore, they keep checking when they're online and activate notifications to know when they share, like, or comment. Outing or doxing is also pretty common and consists of sharing personal information about somebody online. It's extremely dangerous and can have negative consequences in the real world if information like the address is shared with strangers. Other types of cyberbullying you've probably heard about are catfishing, fraping, and dissing. Catfishing occurs when someone lures you into a relationship using a fake persona online, while fraping means using another person's social media account to share harmful content. Dissing involves spreading false information online about someone. As you can see, cyberbullying can take on various shapes, all of which are dangerous.

How can you understand if you or someone you love are experiencing cyberbullying? In general, you might notice they express negative emotions when discussing their online life or using their phone. They might look more nervous and anxious or hesitant when using their devices. They might avoid all forms of social contact, even school or their friends. If you ask them about their online activities, they might refuse to answer and prefer not to talk about it. They might also suffer from depression or anxiety. On the flip side of the coin, how can you understand when someone's being a bully? They usually increase their online activity and have multiple profiles and accounts. They spend a lot of time on social media but never openly discuss what they do. They might also become more concerned about their social status and more aggressive in real life.

Trolling

In the previous section, we discussed a type of cyberbullying called flaming, which involves provoking one person to force them to react and continue the argument. Trolling is very similar to flaming, but it involves more people. Therefore, one person decides to troll an online community, a group of people, and so on to generate conflict. If we don't recognize what the person is doing, we might fall into their trap and continue the online fight. More people might join, and we suddenly find ourselves in a huge, useless argument. In general, people who troll, harass, cyberbully, or attack others. Their favorite discussions include sensitive topics, such as homophobia, racism, misogyny, and all issues that provoke strong reactions in people and create opposite factions. Other times, people who troll use your words against you, take your words out of context, or spam you with offensive content. However, you must keep in mind that not all trolls are the same. Some of them are harmless and just make jokes in good fun. For instance, they might goof around with celebrities or famous brands. In such cases, they don't harm anyone and can create fun social engagement.

How do you recognize if you're dealing with a troll? Both harmless and malicious trolls usually don't make sense and don't stay on topic. They present absurd ideas with an enigmatic language to confuse you and like changing topics to overly silly or random things. For example, they might respond to your messages with completely unrelated images or links. When trolls are petty, you can easily recognize them, thanks to other elements. They make you feel agitated, and you feel like something's off about the conversation you're having with them. They might also call you names and become condescending once you start replying to their messages. When they manage to achieve their goal, and you get angry and react negatively, they start acting surprised to make you believe there's nothing wrong. If they catch you off guard, you might get even more upset and continue the fight. Last but not least, malicious trolls are relentless. While most people just move on with their lives after an online argument, they seem like they'll never stop attacking you. It looks as if their lives revolve around making you feel miserable.

When you realize you're dealing with a troll, you can follow some tips not to fall into their traps and avoid causing useless arguments online. The simplest and most effective way consists of just ignoring them. Even if they call you names, insult you, or use your words against you, don't reply to them. It's more likely that they'll soon stop harassing you if you don't interact with them. However, you might start a conversation with a person and realize only later that they're just a troll. In this case, you can stop talking to them as soon as you realize it, or you can think twice before replying. Choose your words wisely and avoid fueling the argument. Therefore, don't let your emotions write your message, and try to rise above the situation. Don't lose your temper and use words that can help de-escalate the problem. If nothing you try helps you successfully face the troll, you can block them or delete their comments. I'd suggest you block them, as they might become even more aggressive after they realize you deleted their comments.

MAINTAINING A POSITIVE ONLINE PRESENCE

How to Be a Positive Force Online

Now that you know the most common areas of online negativity, let's focus on the bright side. You have the power to foster positivity online by maintaining a positive presence for others. Consider yourself as an example for your loved ones and other followers who might decide to behave in the same way. The first thing you must do to become a positive presence online is clean your list of friends or followers and the accounts you follow. If you've been using social media for some time, you might not even remember all the accounts you follow or that follow you. Check them and look at their posts. If you think they align with your values and spread positive vibes, you can keep following them. If you notice they spread negativity and share offensive content, you must unfollow them. Fill your feed with your loved ones' posts and pictures of cute puppies. That's the best way to become a positive presence.

Once you've cleaned your list of friends and followers, you can start working on the content you share. Think about everything you post, write, and comment on. Do you try to be kind and respectful, or do you often share negative comments? Negativity doesn't only involve insulting others or calling them names. It also includes talking about your life from a negative perspective. For instance, you might keep posting about how you feel stressed, that your life is hard, that you hate school, that nobody loves you, and so on. The above is all negative content that doesn't make your followers feel better. You must become more positive and share the good things that happen to you—no matter how small they are.

The posts you publish on your profile are just as important as your comments. Make sure you carefully choose your words and spread positive vibes. Congratulate your loved ones when something good happens to them, or send them a heart to show you love them and are happy for them. Try to make their day by sharing positive facts about them. You can do the same with strangers who look for help online. If you're part of an online forum or community, you can support other members. Sometimes, people use online platforms to look for advice or find someone who can help them. Leaving a kind comment and encouraging them can make them feel less lonely. You can also positively contribute to online discussions by avoiding escalations, offering your point of view, and respecting others.

This doesn't mean you should stop writing unfriendly comments once and for all. In case of sensitive topics, the conversation might get heated, and you might react more aggressively than you want. Well, it's normal, so you must accept it. Your positive comments should shade all the mean ones. To maintain an online presence, you must also pay attention to the time you spend on social media. After scrolling for a few minutes, you can build up physical and mental tension that can negatively impact your behavior online. The best thing to do is to stop for a while, focus on the parts of your body where you feel the tension, and try to release it. Another way of maintaining a positive online presence is to anonymously report harmful behavior like cyberbullying or trolling. All social media platforms have community standards and offer a way to report those who don't respect them. To make the digital world a better place, you should act against people who harm others. We'll look more in detail at what to do when you witness online negativity in the next section.

What to Do When You Witness Online Negativity

As cyberbullying is pretty common, it might occur to you or one of your loved ones to be bullied. That's why you must be aware of the ways you can protect yourself and the people you care about. Whenever it's possible, it's always better to ignore the bully rather than reply to their mean comments. They usually feel encouraged to keep bullying if they notice a reaction in their victims. At the same time, you must keep track of everything they say or do. Before reporting their behavior, make sure to save all the texts they send you and not delete content that might help others understand how the bully treats you. In fact, it's important that you reach out to someone you trust and feel comfortable talking to. Your parents are usually the recommended figures you should reach out to, but they're not the only ones. If you feel at ease discussing sensitive issues with a teacher, coach, or neighbor, then you should open up to them. The figure you trust should be an adult, but you can also speak to older siblings or friends. If you don't feel like discussing such a sensitive topic with someone you know, you can always count on experts like counselors and psychologists. Once you've gathered enough evidence against the bully, you can block their phone number and their account on social media. The last action you can undertake to fight bullies is to report them to the safety centers of the social media platforms, just like you learned in the previous sections.

If one of your friends tells you they're being bullied or you notice unusual behavior, you can discuss the problem with them. Remember to always be kind, let them talk, and carefully listen to their point of view. Comfort them and help them find out what they can do to stop the bully. Try to understand how they feel and ask them if they feel like reporting the issue to an adult or social media platform. If they look hesitant, ask them why and let them know that they don't need to file an official report but can simply discuss the problem with someone they trust. Keep in mind that your words can make a difference, so choose them wisely.

DIY

Learn the effects of a positive online presence yourself! Choose a social media platform and dedicate a day to only posting positive, uplifting content. Monitor how this impacts your mood and interactions. Reflect on the power of spreading positivity online and how it contributes to a respectful digital environment.

Are you surprised by the effects of the exercise? Is there anything you found particularly interesting when practicing the activity?

In this chapter, we discussed digital etiquette. We learned that following the rules of digital etiquette is essential to ensure we all feel safe online. We also discovered important information about two common forms of online negativity: Cyberbullying and trolling. We learned there are various types of cyberbullying, and they all have serious adverse effects on people's everyday lives. Trolling can sometimes be harmful, and we can deal with it by blocking and ignoring trolls. The most effective way of fighting negativity online is to have a positive online presence. We must spread love among our followers and stop following accounts that share malicious content. In case we notice harmful behavior online, we must report it to an adult we trust or to the social media platform involved. In the next chapter, we'll look at the last strategy we must learn to improve our digital communication: How to become more authentic online.

8

EMBRACING DIGITAL
AUTHENTICITY

Half the world is composed of people who have something to say and can't, and the other half who have nothing to say and keep on saying it.

— ROBERT FROST

I n Chapter 6, I mentioned how important it is to show our vulnerability and be authentic online to improve our relationships. If others know who we truly are, we're also more likely to connect with people who think and feel the same way. Consequently, we're more likely to be appreciated and accepted for who we are. Embracing digital authenticity is essential to building a better digital world and boosting our overall well-being. Faking to be someone different from ourselves won't help us deeply connect and interact with others. In the next sections, we'll learn what authenticity is and why it's essential. We'll also discover why we shouldn't aim at being perfect online and how we can embrace our flaws. Next, we'll discuss why vulnerability is fundamental and how to show it online. Finally, the practical activity at the end of the chapter will help us embrace our true selves online.

AUTHENTICITY

What It Means

Do you ever feel like you're wearing a mask and are hiding your true self? If so, you're not the only one. Sometimes, we feel like we must please others to make them feel happy and appreciated, thus forgetting about ourselves. Alternatively, we feel ashamed of our personality and character, so we try to hide some flaws and behave differently from what we normally would. Such behaviors are the exact opposite of authenticity. Being authentic means expressing and living your true self (Tsaousides, 2023). In other words, your actions align with your values, and you live your life according to your standards, goals, and expectations. If you're not authentic, it means you live based on others' values and objectives. For example, you might care so much about your friends that you choose to go to a specific college with them even if you would have preferred another one or not going at all. Alternatively, you might be influenced by current trends and what society tells you to do, thus hiding your "nerd side" and only showing your extroverted side. These are just examples of what not being authentic looks like. You might believe there's no harm in living your life following others' standards, but that's not true. In fact, going against your values and goals might impact your physical and mental well-being. You might feel stressed, anxious, and tired, and you might hinder your success because you don't express your true potential. As you can see, being authentic can only make your life better.

To understand what authenticity entails, it might help to distinguish it from two similar concepts: Honesty and consistency (Tsaousides, 2023). When you're being honest, you're able to tell the truth. However, we don't always choose to be honest with others for various reasons. For example, we might tell a white lie not to hurt their feelings or decide to withhold the truth because it's too harsh. Alternatively, we can sugarcoat it to help others digest it.

Whenever you decide not to tell the truth, does it mean you're not being authentic? Not at all. Conversely, you're being true to yourself because you decide to withhold the truth to align your behavior with your values. If you value being kind more than being honest, then you're authentic. If you're a consistent person, it means that you tend to behave in the same way in different situations. In other words, your behavior is predictable and, thus, reliable. For example, you might behave in front of your friends just like you would in front of your parents. Therefore, you might consider yourself an authentic person. If you adapt to a different context, you're inconsistent, so you might believe you're not authentic. But that's not true if adjusting your behavior is part of your values and beliefs. If you give importance to adapting to different situations, then you're authentic when you change your behavior depending on the people around you (Tsaousides, 2023).

Why It's Important

Let's look more in detail at why you should aim at being more authentic, especially online. If you're true to your-self, you trust and respect your decisions just like others do. They'll notice you stand by your values and admire you for your choice of showing your real you. You're also more self-aware as you understand what you want and like, what you believe in, and who you are. Consequently, you make the right choices and know exactly what to do in complicated circumstances. You also know how to solve moral dilemmas because your behavior aligns with your values. Consequently, you can face challenges and solve problems more easily. If you're authentic, you don't let others decide what's best for you because you already know it. Therefore, you're free to realize your potential and do what you truly enjoy. Obviously, you must respect others' points of view and value their feedback and advice, but you must also follow your own path. The essential reason why being authentic is important is that it increases your confidence and self-esteem, which allows you to achieve all your goals and live a fulfilling life. Finally, if you're authentic, you also feel less stressed because you don't have to force yourself to think and do as others would. You can say what you mean, stay true to yourself, and behave accordingly. Can you imagine how your life could be if you were completely authentic?

ONLINE PERFECTIONISM

You Don't Have to Be Perfect Online

The reason most people struggle to be authentic online is social pressure. Whenever we look at Instagram, TikTok, Snapchat, and other social media platforms, we're bombarded with perfect pictures of people having fun, enjoying their lives, and living the dream. It seems like everybody's having a good time except us. We look at their pictures and envy them for their bodies and popularity. They look perfect while we're not. And that's exactly when we decide to leave behind authenticity to show others we live a satisfying life, too. We use filters to embellish our pictures, and we carefully choose quotes and words to appear wise and deep.

But are others truly living such an enviable life? Have you ever thought that, as you try to beautify your life, so do other people? I'm sure nobody is completely satisfied and lives peacefully. Think about all the cute couples you follow that post amazing pictures where they kiss and look perfect. Do you really think they're all so happy? You can't know what happens behind the scenes. They might have argued for hours and made peace just a few minutes before taking the picture. Or they might start arguing because one partner always likes posting stuff on their account while the other would like them to stop. One thing we tend to forget while scrolling social media is that we just see what others want us to see, which usually is the most superficial and stress-free part of their lives. We don't know what's happening in their real lives. They might struggle with anxiety, have the same fears we have, and crave to be perfect.

How to Be Yourself and Embrace Flaws

Deciding to hide your true self to appear perfect in front of others is simply useless and counterproductive. Nobody's perfect, and there's nothing wrong in showing who you really are. We all have bad days, times when we even struggle to get out of bed, and flaws we wouldn't want to have. But we're just human beings and can do nothing about it. To live a truly satisfying life, you must be yourself and embrace your flaws. But how can you do it?

First of all, you must stop comparing yourself to others. You don't know everything about them, what they've been through, the obstacles they faced, and why they decided to post amazing pictures on their profiles every day. Therefore, it doesn't make sense to compare yourself to them. You live a different life and have different friends, family, and opportunities. Secondly, you must realize craving perfectionism leads to frustration, as you'll never be perfect. If you want to be happy, you must let go of the idea of being perfect. If you think about it, what is defined as perfect is determined by movies, ads, and television characters. In other words, society decides what's perfect and what's not. Do you want to live by the standards of society or by yours? Next, you must take inspiration from famous works of art. Do you know that perfect symmetry is often boring? The finest works of art aren't perfect but convey emotions, which is the essential aspect that makes them so magnificent. Similarly, our flaws make us interesting because they convey emotions.

Another thing you should do every time you think about your flaws and wish you'd never had them is to balance them. Are you only made of flaws, or do you also have some strengths? Like all of us, you have plenty of qualities that make others love and admire you. If you don't manage to find them, just ask around. Your parents, friends, and classmates will surely surprise you by telling you all the qualities they think you have. Finally, you can be yourself and embrace your flaws by flipping or reframing them. What makes you feel miserable is also what makes you strong and special. Let's imagine you think you have two horrible flaws: You're both shy and quiet. Now, try to flip them. If you're shy and quiet, it means you're an amazing observer and listener. No matter what your flaws are—they all have a flip side.

ON BEING VULNERABLE

Why Being Vulnerable Online Is a Good Thing

When we discussed authenticity and embracing your flaws in the previous sections, you might have immediately thought about vulnerability. In fact, being authentic and showing your weaknesses means being vulnerable, and we all know how much we hate it. We would all want to appear powerful and invincible. But if we all want the same thing, doesn't it indicate we're all vulnerable in reality? Yes, it does. As perfectionism, invincibility doesn't exist. Conversely, vulnerability is a strength. Society makes us believe being vulnerable means being fearful and uncertain, thus making others more likely to reject us or leading us to failure. For all the above reasons, we tend to perceive vulnerability as a weakness even if it isn't.

Being vulnerable implies being authentic and showing others your true self. It also improves your relationships and boosts intimacy because others see you for who you truly are. If you show your flaws and fears to others, they'll be more likely to open up with you and perceive your relationship as deep and strong. They'll feel comfortable talking to you and admire you for your choice to be yourself in a world where everyone tries to be someone else. Therefore, vulnerability also builds empathy and allows us to properly process and express our emotions. If we think we must look invincible and never show our struggles, we don't elaborate on our emotions and hide them inside of us. One day, they might reappear and become problematic. If we embrace vulnerability, we're not afraid of reflecting on our emotions—positive and negative ones—and asking for help from others or discussing them with our loved ones.

We must accept that vulnerability is a part of everyone's lives. We're all vulnerable and have flaws. You might feel terrified to show vulnerability by saying "I love you," trying a new experience, or sharing a struggle you've recently had. Although you might think you'll do better if you keep those thoughts to yourself, you'll get rewarded in the long run. You might discover the person you love loves you back and was waiting for you to tell them that a new experience is extremely funny, and someone faced your same struggle and can help you.

How to Engage With Vulnerability Online

If you've never been vulnerable in front of others and want to give it a try, you might wonder where you can start from. Here, you find a few tips that might help you recover from your fear of being vulnerable. The first thing you must learn is to be authentic and love yourself. Once you accept yourself for who you are and appreciate all your strengths and weaknesses, you can embrace your vulnerability. I know it might look scary as you've probably been hurt in the past and don't want to feel hurt again. But if you close yourself off, it's more likely you will struggle to find someone who appreciates you for who you are and is willing to build a deep relationship. Another trick that helps you embrace vulnerability is to treat yourself as you treat others. If your best friend fails an exam, do you mock them and tell them they're stupid? I guess not. You'd probably comfort them and tell them they'll do better next time. Are you able to say the same things to yourself? If not, start doing it. Every time you beat yourself up because of a mistake or failure, ask yourself what you would do if your best friend were in the same situation. Then, tell yourself what you'd tell them. The real secret is aiming for excellence, not perfection. You can always improve, but you'll never be perfect.

To embrace your vulnerability, you must also learn to express what you need, want, and think. Have you ever wanted to please someone and agreed with them to avoid conflict and show your true self? Well, it happens to all of us. However, we don't feel happier or improve our relationships. We must clearly express what we need and what we think. Moreover, we must learn to say what we want from others instead of what we don't want or like. Many relationships fall apart because people only focus on the negative aspects and say what they don't like about the other person. When they change their viewpoint and focus on what they want, they start feeling more empathetic.

What about online? There are specific ways in which you can embrace vulnerability online. For example, you can use your camera more often. You can take videos or make stories about yourself without using filters. You can also share short videos of you dancing or doing silly stuff on TikTok. Even when you're making new friends online, you can decide to make video calls instead of just chatting. You shouldn't be afraid of showing yourself and your room to others, as they also have flaws and things they don't like about themselves. If you try to use your camera more often, make sure to do it gradually. Start with something you feel comfortable with, and then slowly try more frightening activities.

DIY

Do you want to find out how authentic you are online? Collect images, quotes, and words that represent different facets of your personality. Create a digital collage that showcases your authentic self. Share it with a close friend or on a private social media platform and encourage them to do the same. Reflect on the experience of embracing your true self online.

In this last chapter, we focused on authenticity. We discovered that it's essential to boost our relationships with others and improve our mental and physical health. Next, we learned that perfectionism is the opposite of authenticity and makes our lives worse. If we want to feel happy and satisfied, we must learn to embrace our flaws and vulnerability. Showing our true selves and weaknesses to others creates deep and strong connections. Finally, we looked at an easy activity that shows us how authentic we are on social media. In this chapter, we looked at the last strategy that helps us improve our digital communication. The last thing left to do is to put into practice everything we've learned and try the activities we found in each chapter (if we haven't yet). Now, we have all the tools to successfully use social media platforms and digital communication to boost our relationships and increase our physical and mental health.

YOUR MISSION SHOULD YOU CHOOSE TO ACCEPT IT...

Your online communication skills have been given a boost ... but as we all know, communication is a two-way street, and we need as many people as possible to acquire these same skills. This is your chance to spread the word!

Simply by sharing your honest opinion of this book and a little about your own journey, you'll show new readers where they can find everything they need to sharpen their online communication skills just like you have.

IN UNDER 1 MINUTE
YOU CAN HELP OTHERS JUST LIKE YOU BY LEAVING A REVIEW!

Thank you so much for your support. Now, get out there and spread the love!

Scan the QR code below

CONCLUSION

Let's go back to the beginning when you might have thought books aren't for you and you already know everything you need about social media and technology. Do you still believe it, or did you learn something new in the above pages? I'm pretty sure you feel surprised, and you've learned many interesting facts and tried funny activities.

In the first chapter, we introduced the concept of digital communication and looked at its pros and cons. On one hand, digital communication improves our lives by helping us make new friends online and connect with people around the world. On the other hand, it can be confusing because we have too many channels to choose from, we lack essential non-verbal cues to understand what others mean, and we feel the urge to always be available online. In the second chapter, we dived deep into the topic of digital communication and discussed two common lost messengers: Tone and context. The main problem with texts is that we struggle to understand the meaning of words because we can't infer the tone and context. In other words, we don't understand if the person who texts us is being sarcastic or serious and what is the main context of the conversation. The negative consequence of losing such important messengers is a misunderstanding, which occurs when the sender doesn't manage to successfully convey a message and the receiver doesn't interpret it properly. To recover the lost messengers and avoid misunderstandings, we can use some straightforward strategies to read between the lines, pick up common patterns, and infer emotions from the text. For example, we can use emojis to help others understand how we feel.

In Chapter 3, we kept discussing emojis and their pros and cons. They can help us understand others' feelings but, at the same time, can cause misunderstandings. In fact, we don't all give the same meaning to the same emoji, and expressing emotions is already hard with words—imagine with little faces on small screens. If we want to effectively use emojis, we should limit them to the most common and less ambiguous ones, like the smiley face, and add just one emoji at the end of our message. To properly express and understand our and others' emotions, we can also use other strategies. We can expand our vocabulary so that we learn more words to express how we feel, we can use the emotion wheel to understand the intensity and depth of our emotions, or we can use descriptive language to add details to our texts. In Chapter 3, we also looked at some funny activities we can try by ourselves or with our loved ones to practice how to understand and express emotions. In Chapter 4, we discovered the importance of empathy and how we can develop it. To show empathy, we must be completely honest with others and show them we care by using sentences like, "I'm here for you." We also learned how to recognize and respond to emotional cues over text, and we looked at situations in which we can try to show more empathy toward others.

In the fifth chapter, we focused on conflicts online and how we can see them as opportunities to learn something new. In fact, not all conflicts are negative: Some of them can improve and deepen our relationships. To properly solve conflicts, we must listen before talking, use "I" statements to avoid making others feel attacked, get to the roots of the problem, and find an agreement together. If everything we do doesn't solve the issue, then we must simply drop it and walk away. In Chapter 5, we also looked at step-by-step guides on how to give, receive, and implement feedback. In Chapter 6, we discussed relationships and how difficult it is to build deep connections online. It doesn't mean that it's impossible. The secret is to blend online and offline communication, as we all crave human contact and physical interaction. If we regularly keep in touch with our online friends and organize meetings in our presence from time to time, it's more likely that we'll build strong and deep relationships. We also looked at some successful and heartbreaking stories of people who met online and became best friends for life.

In Chapter 7, we discovered that the digital world has etiquette, too, and we must follow the rules to make sure everyone safely navigates the internet and builds a healthy digital world. The most common areas of negativity online are cyberbullying and trolling, which can be extremely dangerous and harmful. In fact, they can both have an impact on our real lives. That's why we must never cyberbully or troll someone online and do something in case we notice such behaviors. For example, we can report them to the social media platform involved, or we can block them. To improve the digital world, we can spread good vibes by sharing positive and uplifting posts, showing love to our followers, and helping others seeking online support. In Chapter 8, we focused on authenticity and vulnerability, which are essential to living a happy and fulfilling life and improving our relationships. If we show others who we truly are, they're more likely to do the same and accept us. We're also more likely to build deep connections.

In this book, we looked at some interesting facts about digital communication and strategies to become more effective at using it. Thanks to all the practical tips and activities, you can make your life better. Commit yourself to spreading love online and making meaningful connections. Take what you've learned and put it to the test—get out there and communicate with style, navigating your phone like never before! You've got this.

REFERENCES

Ackerman, C. E. (2019, May 27). 49 communication activities, exercises & games. Positive Psychology. https://positivepsychology.com/communication-games-and-activities/#google_vignette

Albritton, A. (2017). Emotions in the ether: strategies for effective emotional expression in text-messages. Online Journal of Communication and Media Technologies, 7(2). https://doi.org/10.29333/ojcmt/2590

Anderson, M., & Jiang, J. (2018, May 31). *Teens, social media & technology*. Pew Research Center. https://www.pewresearch.org/internet/2018/05/31/teens-social-media-technology-2018/

Atchison, J. (2020, January 9). *How to build real friendships online*. Thrive Global. https://community.thriveglobal.com/how-to-build-real-friendships-online/#:

Authenticity. (n.d.). MindTools. https://www.mindtools.com/ay30irc/authenticity

Blending online and offline communications. (2022, October 14). Success Quarterly. https://successquarterly.com/blending-online-and-offline-communications/?utm_content=cmp-true

Brown, B. (2023, July 6). *16 signs you're naturally good at empathizing with others*. The Expert Editor. https://experteditor.com.au/blog/signs-youre-naturally-good-at-empathizing-with-others/

Building and maintaining healthy relationships. (2021, October 27). Health Direct. https://www.healthdirect.gov.au/building-and-maintaining-healthy-relationships

Calvello, M. (2022, March 10). *How to implement feedback as a manager in 5 steps*. Fellow. https://fellow.app/blog/feedback/how-to-implement-feedback-as-a-manager/

Camberato, J. (2023, February 17). *Are apps enough for effective office communication?* Forbes. https://www.forbes.com/sites/forbesfinancecouncil/2023/02/17/are-apps-enough-for-effective-office-communication/?sh=3dd83bf661b1

Carefoot, H. (2023, January 12). *6 physical cues to walk away from an argument, according to a body language expert*. Well+Good. https://www.wellandgood.com/when-to-walk-away-from-argument/

Carnduff, C. (2023, May 12). *Exploring the disadvantages of virtual communication*. Coffee Pals. https://www.coffeepals.com/blog/exploring-the-disadvantages-of-virtual-communication

Ciarkowski, C. (2022, November 15). *When emotions run high, here's how to respond*. Accelerate Learning Community. https://accelerate.uofuhealth.utah.edu/resilience/when-emotions-run-high-here-s-how-to-respond

Clarke, T. (2019, February 28). *Squash social media trolls with these 9 tips [guide]*. Hootsuite. https://blog.hootsuite.com/how-to-deal-with-trolls-on-social-media/

Click, L. (2021, August 21). *31 empathetic statements for when you don't know what to say*. Medium. https://medium.com/@lauraclick/31-empathetic-statements-for-when-you-dont-know-what-to-say-edd50822c96a

Collins, D. (n.d.). *Evaluating news: digital etiquette*. LibGuide. https://libguides.trschools.k12.wi.us/evaluatingnews/netiquette#:

Conaway, C. (2022, June 14). *The right way to process feedback*. Harvard Business Review. https://hbr.org/2022/06/the-right-way-to-process-feedback

Cooks-Campbell, A. (2022, April 20). *The emotion wheel: how to use it to get to know yourself*. Better Up. https://www.betterup.com/blog/emotion-wheel

Cutolo, M. (2023, August 3). *12 texting habits you might not realize are annoying*. Reader's Digest. https://www.rd.com/list/annoying-texting-habits/

Cyberbullying: what is it and how to stop it. (2023, February). UNICEF. https://www.unicef.org/end-violence/how-to-stop-cyberbullying

Davis, T. (2016, April 29). *6 tips for reading emotions in text messages*. Mindful. https://www.mindful.org/six-tips-reading-emotions-text-messages/

Descriptive writing. (n.d.). Reading Rockets. https://www.readingrockets.org/classroom/classroom-strategies/descriptive-writing#:

Digital etiquette. (2016, February 17). Eduwebinar. https://eduwebinar. com.au/digital-etiquette/#:

Effective email communication. (2019). University of North Carolina at Chapel Hill. https://writingcenter.unc.edu/tips-and-tools/effec tive-e-mail-communication/

Empathy. (2019). Psychology Today. https://www.psychologytoday. com/us/basics/empathy

Evbuomwan, O. (2022, February 14). *How to be intentional about building authentic relationships*. Medium. https://theroomworldwide. medium.com/how-to-be-intentional-about-building-authentic-rela tionships-913a25387201

Feintuch, S. (2020, November 12). *10 signs you have incredible empathy*. The Healthy. https://www.thehealthy.com/mental-health/have-empathy/

Firestone, L. (2017, June 22). *How embracing vulnerability strengthens our relationships*. PsychAlive. https://www.psychalive.org/embracing-vulnerability-strengthens-connections/

5 benefits of healthy relationships. (2021, September). Northwestern Medicine. https://www.nm.org/healthbeat/healthy-tips/5-bene fits-of-healthy-relationships

5 ways to embrace your flaws and rewrite your life. (2021, November 30). Tri-MED. https://www.trimedhealth.com/5-ways-embrace-flaws-rewrite-your-life/

Fritscher, L. (2019). *Overcoming a fear of vulnerability and love your imperfections*. Verywell Mind. https://www.verywellmind.com/fear-of-vulnerability-2671820

Gilbert, K. (2022, February 11). *5 tone of voice examples and tips to improve your messaging*. Gather Content. https://gathercontent.com/ blog/a-simple-tool-to-guide-tone-of-voice

Grimes-Viort, B. (2011, May 19). *16 causes of conflict in an online commu-nity*. Social Media Today. https://www.socialmediatoday.com/ content/16-causes-conflict-online-community

Hess, W. (2012, August 21). *On empathy and apathy: two case studies*. Whitney Hess. https://whitneyhess.com/blog/2012/08/21/on-empathy-and-apathy-two-case-studies/

Hirschlag, A. (2017, May 15). *4 awesome "how we met" friendship stories that will inspire you to get online.* Up Worthy. https://www.upworthy.com/4-awesome-how-we-met-friendship-stories-that-will-inspire-you-to-get-online

Holland, J. (2017, October 17). *The problem with emojis.* Joseph Greenwald & Laake, PA. https://www.jgllaw.com/blog/problem-emojis

How to give feedback that motivates & engages. (n.d.). Leapsome. https://www.leapsome.com/blog/how-to-give-feedback-in-5-steps

How to show empathy over text communication. (2022, May 11). OhMD. https://www.ohmd.com/how-to-show-empathy-over-text-communication/

The importance of connection and empathy. (2022, April 29). The Master Series. https://themasterseries.com/the-importance-of-connection-and-empathy/

The importance of vocabulary. (n.d.). JCFS Chicago. https://www.jcfs.org/blog/importance-vocabulary#:

Jolly, J. (n.d.). *Your guide on how to use emojis.* USA TODAY. https://eu.usatoday.com/story/tech/personal/2015/11/15/your-guide-how-use-emojis/75771850/

Khanorkar, S. (2023, February 28). *Empathy: the power of understanding and connecting with others.* LinkedIn. https://www.linkedin.com/pulse/empathy-power-understanding-connecting-others-samrat-khanorkar/

Lelwica Buttaccio, J. (2022, December 20). *8 ways to turn your online friends into real-life besties.* Reader's Digest. https://www.rd.com/list/online-friends/

Levine, J. A. (2019, March 8). *The trouble with emojis.* Lexology. https://www.lexology.com/library/detail.aspx?g=d0dfa787-753d-4dac-9d16-45b83e75fb4d

Lockett, E. (2022, December 7). *Everything you need to know about cyberbullying.* Healthline. https://www.healthline.com/health/mental-health/cyberbullying

Lorenz, T. (2021, August 15). Now going viral: meeting online friends in real life. *The New York Times.* https://www.nytimes.com/2021/08/15/technology/tik-tok-friends-meet-up.html

Maintain healthy relationships. (2016). Mental Health Foundation.

https://www.wechu.org/sites/default/files/workplace%20wellness/
ease%20your%20mind/relationship_ebulletin_FINAL.PDF

Marie, S. (2022, August 26). *9 ways to solve misunderstandings in a relationship.* Psych Central. https://psychcentral.com/relationships/
pointers-for-couples-to-prevent-resolve-misunderstandings

Maton, K. (2021, October 27). *6 benefits of digital communication you can't ignore.* Datagraphic. https://datagraphic.co.uk/news/benefits-of-digital-communication/

Menjivar, J. (n.d.). *8 ways to make the internet a more positive place.* DoSomething.org. https://www.dosomething.org/us/articles/
ways-to-make-the-internet-a-more-positive-place

Miles, M. (2022, March 25). *Are you receptive to feedback? Follow this step-by-step guide.* Better Up. https://www.betterup.com/blog/receptive-to-feedback

Miscommunication: the problem with texting. (n.d.). Scribendi. https://www.scribendi.com/academy/articles/miscommunica
tion_and_texting.en.html#:

Patrick, M. (n.d.). *How to know when to walk away from a conflict at work.* Chron. https://smallbusiness.chron.com/walk-away-conflict-work-21306.html

Pitagorsky, G. (2018, August 24). *Communicating your understanding.* PM Times. https://www.projecttimes.com/articles/communicat
ing-your-understanding/#:

Positive conflict: 4 benefits of positive conflict in the workplace. (2022, April 14). MasterClass. https://www.masterclass.com/articles/posi
tive-conflict

Practice effective communication with texting activities. (n.d.). Human Kinetics. https://us.humankinetics.com/blogs/excerpt/practice-effective-communication-with-texting-activities

Rauv, S. (2021, June 15). *15 essential apps for workplace collaboration and communication.* Elcom. https://www.elcom.com.au/resources/blog/
15-essential-communication-platforms-and-software-to-use

Receiving and giving effective feedback. (2019). University of Waterloo. https://uwaterloo.ca/centre-for-teaching-excellence/cata
logs/tip-sheets/receiving-and-giving-effective-feedback

Reid, S. (2023, March 22). *Empathy.* Https://Www.helpguide.org.

https://www.helpguide.org/articles/relationships-communication/empathy.htm

Reilly, M. (2023, January 30). *3 techniques for turning vulnerability into connection online*. Scaling Intimacy. https://scalingintimacy.com/blog/turning-vulnerability-into-connection-blog/

Roberts, G. (n.d.). *Context and tone*. Word Perfect. https://www.wordperfect.com/en/pages/items/1600108.html#:

Roullier, A. (2022, January 2). *Don't be fooled by social media. Not everyone is living their best life*. The Authentic Optimist. https://theauthenticoptimist.com/dont-be-fooled-not-everyone-is-living-their-best-life/

Russell, G. (2021, June 25). *Understanding tone: your audience deserves context*. Self-Publishing School. https://self-publishingschool.com/understanding-tone/

Seager, T. P. (2019, June 25). *Communications in the digital age is confusing*. Medium. https://medium.com/p/adf1d6f8542d

Seiter, C. (2016, August 10). *The psychology of social media: why we like, comment, and share online*. Buffer. https://buffer.com/resources/psychology-of-social-media/

Selby. (2023, August 21). *Texting miscommunication: causes, effects, and solutions*. Everyday Speech. https://everydayspeech.com/sel-implementation/texting-miscommunication-causes-effects-and-solutions/

7 benefits of digital communication in the workplace. (2022, February 4). Evolvous. https://evolvous.com/digital-communication-benefits-in-workplace/7-benefits/

Shrayber, M. (2023, August 3). *Two best friends meet in real life for the first time*. Up Worthy. https://www.upworthy.com/they-only-knew-each-other-online-they-finally-met-in-real-life-and-it-was-amazing-rp2

6 key benefits of digital communication in the workplace. (2022, November 3). Workest. https://www.zenefits.com/workest/benefits-of-digital-communication-in-the-workplace/

Spoelma, J. (2018, June 17). *Communication breakdown: how misunderstandings happen and what to do about it*. Career Foresight Coaching.

https://careerforesight.co/blog-feed/communication-breakdown-how-misunderstandings-happen-and-what-to-do-about-it

Tan, R. (2021, October 7). *Emojis and accessibility: how to use them properly.* Medium. https://uxdesign.cc/emojis-in-accessibility-how-to-use-them-properly-66b73986b803

10 easy ways to improve your vocabulary skills. (2023, February 17). Indeed. https://www.indeed.com/career-advice/career-development/improve-vocabulary-skills

The 10 most essential digital communication channels for business. (2022, November 21). Talkative. https://gettalkative.com/info/communication-channels

"The 50 Most Captivating Quotes About Social Media And Mental Health." Vantage Fit - A Complete Solution To Your Corporate Wellness Program. Last modified May 17, 2023. https://www.vantagefit.io/blog/quotes-about-social-media-and-mental-health/.

Texting etiquette: context, tone and timing matters. (2019, June 4). WRAL News. https://www.wral.com/story/texting-etiquette-context-tone-and-timing-matters/18430623/

35 quotes about communication for inspiring team collaboration. (2022, May 5). Vibe. https://vibe.us/blog/35-quotes-about-communication/

Tone in text messages. (n.d.). Cyber Definitions. https://www.cyberdefinitions.com/tone_indicators_in_texting.html

Tracy, B. (2018, September 20). *How to improve your vocabulary for writing & speaking success.* Brian Tracy International. https://www.briantracy.com/blog/writing/how-to-improve-your-vocabulary/

Tsaousides, T. (2023, August 10). *What it means to be truly authentic.* Psychology Today. https://www.psychologytoday.com/us/blog/smashing-the-brainblocks/202211/what-it-means-to-be-truly-authentic

Understanding other people. (2011). Skills You Need. https://www.skillsyouneed.com/ips/understanding-others.html

Verhoff, E. (2012, October 23). *10 tips for embracing your flaws.* SheKnows. https://www.sheknows.com/health-and-wellness/articles/973125/10-tips-for-embracing-your-flaws/

Wayne, D. (2022, September 10). *How social media pressure to be perfect is making millennials stressed and anxious*. Online Anxiety Therapy. https://www.millennialtherapy.com/anxiety-therapy-blog/social-media-pressure-to-be-perfect

What digital communication mistakes do you need to avoid? (n.d.). Linkedin. https://www.linkedin.com/advice/1/what-digital-communication-mistakes#:

What is communication? (2011). Skills You Need. https://www.skillsyouneed.com/ips/what-is-communication.html

What is digital etiquette? (2019). Digital Citizenship. http://millerdigitalcitizenship.weebly.com/digital-etiquette.html

What is empathy? (2011). Skills You Need. https://www.skillsyouneed.com/ips/empathy.html

What to do if you're a victim. (n.d.). Delete Cyberbullying. https://www.endcyberbullying.net/what-to-do-if-youre-a-victim

Why it's important to practise digital etiquette. (2019, June 15). Borneo Post. https://www.theborneopost.com/2019/06/15/why-its-important-to-practise-digital-etiquette/

Why vulnerability is a strength. (2021, May 13). Eugene Therapy. https://eugenetherapy.com/article/why-vulnerability-is-a-strength/

Wiebe, J. (2019, August 29). *Why is it important to be vulnerable?* Talkspace. https://www.talkspace.com/blog/why-important-to-be-vulnerable/

Wu, O. (2021, June 16). *The only way to form meaningful relationships with people who get you.* Tiny Buddha. https://tinybuddha.com/blog/the-only-way-to-form-meaningful-relationships-with-people-who-get-you/

Zofi, Y. (2020, March 27). *How to resolve the most common conflicts on virtual teams.* HarperCollins Leadership Essentials. https://hcleadershipessentials.com/blogs/team-development/how-to-resolve-the-most-common-conflicts-on-virtual-teams#:

IMAGES REFERENCES

Bach, B. (2021). *Latin American couple at table with textbooks with smart-phones* [Image]. Pexels. https://www.pexels.com/photo/latin-ameri can-couple-at-table-with-textbooks-with-smartphones-6532612/

Burrow, J. (2021). *Collage of smartphones with woman portrait on surface* [Image]. Pexels. https://www.pexels.com/photo/collage-of-smart phones-with-woman-portrait-on-surface-6858618/

Casiano, S. (2018). *Hi haters scrabble tiles on white surface* [Image]. Pexels. https://www.pexels.com/photo/hi-haters-scrabble-tiles-on-white-surface-944743/

Chan, A. (2017). *This is the sign you've been looking for* [Image]. Unsplash. https://unsplash.com/it/foto/ukzHlkoz1IE

Cottonbro Studio. (2020). *Person writing on blackboard with chalk* [Image]. Pexels. https://www.pexels.com/photo/person-writing-on-black-board-with-chalk-3825306/

Cottonbro Studio. (2020). *Photo of person's hands* [Image]. Pexels. https://www.pexels.com/photo/photo-of-person-s-hands-4631065/

Finn. (2020). *Brown concrete building during the day* [Image]. Unsplash. https://unsplash.com/it/foto/nJupV3AOP-U

Google DeepMind. (2023). *Climate, technology, research, energy* [Image]. Pexels. https://unsplash.com/it/foto/SYTO3xs06fU

Hill, P. T. (2021). *Purple and white happy birthday card* [Image]. Pexels. https://www.pexels.com/photo/handwritten-love-books-writing-6537124/

Madeline, E. (2022). *A woman standing on a beach next to a body of water* [Image]. *Unsplash. https://unsplash.com/it/foto/V4GN2eu4OpM*

Mart Production. (2021). *A woman vlogging while sitting on a couch* [Image]. Pexels. https://www.pexels.com/photo/a-woman-vlog ging-while-sitting-on-a-couch-7481942/

Monstera Production. (2020). *Man on a video call* [Image]. Pexels. https://www.pexels.com/photo/man-on-a-video-call-5996855/

Odintsov, R. (2021). *Yellow painted eggs with various facial expressions* [Image]. Pexels. https://www.pexels.com/photo/yellow-painted-eggs-with-various-facial-expressions-6898861/

P, O. (2022). *Hand stopping domino effect* [Image]. Pexels. https://www.pexels.com/photo/hand-stopping-domino-effect-12955678/

Pixabay. (2016). *Art kit wallpaper* [Image]. Pexels. https://www.pexels.com/photo/art-kit-wallpaper-207666/

Priyampatel4. (2020). *Starbucks coffee drink cafe food* [Image]. Pixabay. https://pixabay.com/photos/starbucks-coffee-drink-cafe-food-5085117/

Shuraeva, A. (2020). *Fashion love people woman* [Image]. Pexels. https://www.pexels.com/photo/fashion-love-people-woman-6015524/

Shvets, A. (2020). *Photo of people reaching each others hands* [Image]. Pexels. https://www.pexels.com/photo/photo-of-people-reaching-each-other-s-hands-4672714/

Skitterphoto. (2016). *High rise building with lights* [Image]. Pexels. https://www.pexels.com/photo/high-rise-building-with-lights-42414/

Summer, L. (2021). *Concerned woman browsing smartphone in room* [Image]. Pexels. https://www.pexels.com/photo/concerned-woman-browsing-smartphone-in-room-6383268/